# SUMMER FURNITURE

# SUMMER FURNITURE

## PRACTICAL DESIGNS FOR THE BACKYARD

TOM CARPENTER · CAMDEN HOUSE
ILLUSTRATIONS BY ROBERTA COOKE

**Canadian Cataloguing in Publication Data**

Carpenter, Thomas, 1959 -
    Summer furniture : practical designs for the backyard

Includes index.
ISBN 0-921820-89-5

1. Outdoor furniture.    I. Title.

TT197.5.09C37  1994    684.1'8    C94-931195-2

Printed and bound in Canada by
Metropole Litho Inc.
St. Bruno de Montarville, Quebec

Published by Camden House Publishing
(a division of Telemedia Communications Inc.)

Camden House Publishing
7 Queen Victoria Road
Camden East, Ontario K0K 1J0

Camden House Publishing
Box 766
Buffalo, New York 14240-0766

Printed and distributed under exclusive licence from
Telemedia Communications Inc. by
Firefly Books
250 Sparks Avenue
Willowdale, Ontario
Canada M2H 2S4

Firefly Books (U.S.) Inc.
P.O. Box 1338
Ellicott Station
Buffalo, New York 14205

Design by
Linda J. Menyes

Cover photograph by
Ernie Sparks

Cover photograph: Location and plants courtesy Neil's Flowers, Kingston, Ontario; Bricks courtesy Patterson Concrete Products, Kingston, Ontario.

## ACKNOWLEDGEMENTS

In this book, I have tried to present woodworking not as an exact science, in which you simply follow instructions, but rather as a process that involves thinking carefully about what you want to accomplish and then talking it over with everyone you can find who might be able to help you shape your plans. I am fortunate to have friends and acquaintances who were always willing to listen and to suggest innovations, who now and then reminded me of the basic rules of cut and screw and paste and who tempered my enthusiasm tactfully. I would like to thank David Carr-Harris, Mansor Ghoreshy, Doug Casnaw, Terry Gibson, Peter Dundas, Jeff Taylor, Merilyn Simonds Mohr, Wayne Grady, Steve Dennis and Bob Garvey, each of whom, in his or her own way, helped me to design and assemble the projects contained in these pages. I'd also like to thank Barry Vankoughnet, who filled in the gaps for me after I'd already asked everyone else about paints.

For their part in the infinitely more complex task of assembling this book, thanks to my editor Michael Webster and to the Camden House staff: art director Linda Menyes, editor Tracy Read, assistant editor Catherine DeLury, production manager Susan Dickinson and associate Mary Patton. A special thanks to Roberta Cooke for her wonderful illustrations and to Sandy Taylor for her many suggestions and for her encouragement from the outset.

Finally, I would like to thank all those people who tested Adirondack chairs for me; that list includes most of the people I know.

# CONTENTS

Outdoor furniture is everything that indoor furniture is not, which explains much of its appeal: you can walk on it, spill stuff on it, let the kids turn it upside down and build forts with it. You can even allow it to fall apart in the weather, because somehow the paint peeling from a deck chair only adds to its charm. And since outdoor furniture is never upholstered, you can almost always figure out what holds it up and how the builder put it together—and that explains the rest of its appeal.

Even people who do not usually spend a lot of time in a woodworking shop like to think they can knock together a table and some chairs for the deck—and so they can. Building outdoor furniture is what workaholic executives do in the first year of retirement and everyone else tries long before then. Next to bookshelves, a bench is probably the most common home project.

Yet for the person who has decided to furnish the yard, there is surprisingly little good published material offering simple patterns and techniques. The books that are available usually provide a couple of introductory projects—perhaps on the theory that people will use them as a warmup—then move up a steep learning curve to a level of cabinetry detail that requires significant experience or sophisticated power tools or infinite patience—sometimes all three. Most readers meet the learning curve after only one or two projects and move from there into discouragement. There are also numerous books of simpler projects, but they often lack the kinds of illustration and text that you need to start from scratch and produce furniture; they perhaps assume that if you don't want fancy furniture, then you probably won't want much instruction either.

This book keeps things consistently simple. It discusses a couple of types of chairs and a variety of benches and tables, as well as a planter and a few odds and ends. In each case, the text goes beyond a basic list of the how-to stages of assembly and describes the principles involved, and I hope this accomplishes a couple of things: that it makes the instructions easier to understand and that it provides the reader with what she or he needs to know to be able to modify or redesign the plans. Instead of a collection of recipes for weekend projects, the instructions for specific pieces are used as the starting points for discussions of how to build certain kinds of furniture. You can take it from there.

This book is aimed at do-it-yourselfers who trust their own abilities but have neither the experience nor the well-equipped workshop necessary to do traditional joinery. The techniques and styles suggested assume that the reader does not mind spending a bit of money on materials and that aesthetics and quality take priority over economy. (Chairs and tables can be assembled entirely from exterior-grade plywood; while fast and inexpensive, they look decidedly odd.) I have also kept in mind that most of us make mistakes and that, when we do, it is better to know how to adjust and move on than to throw away materials and have to start again.

Modification is not just the soul of outdoor furniture design, it's the whole thing. There are, for instance, a zillion ways to build a bench, and if you look around, it seems that almost all of them have been tried. The puzzling form of the chair on your great-uncle's verandah probably sprang from a pile of scrap materials that were just a little too good to throw away. And the weird design of the table at your friend's cottage can likely be traced to a sunny Saturday morning when the builder started the day by carefully cutting all the materials just a bit too short on one end.

Along with the assumptions about readers' skills and level of experience, this book also supposes that most of you do not have the shop space to dry your own wood and are therefore dependent on the local lumberyard and the wood you can find there. The management of moisture in wood is an engineering science with a long tradition, and you can find as much information on the subject and as many opinions as your interest will absorb. In the meantime, keep in mind that if a bone-dry plank gets rained on, it will get bigger. If you nail two such pieces together and they get rained on, they will push on each other until something gives. On the other hand, a damp piece of wood sitting outside on a hot sunny day shrinks. Both the designs and the instructions included here anticipate that the wood

# A NOTE ABOUT DIMENSIONS

More than one factor conspires against the wood-worker who tries to build with wood purchased at a lumberyard, and many of those factors have to do with the unpredictable sizes of the material sold there.

For starters, nothing, except plywood, is what it says it is. A 4x8 sheet of ¾-inch ply is, just as one might expect, 4 feet wide by 8 feet long by ¾ inch thick. What it's called and what it is are one and the same thing. For lumber, however, the names we use are just labels. The designation 2x4 is just a term for something that usually—but not always—measures 1⅝ by 3⅝ inches.

Lumber used to fall from the saw blade an honest and true size. A rough-cut 2x4 measured 2 inches by 4 inches. If you wanted it "dressed," it passed through a planer of one sort or another, emerging much smoother and somewhat smaller. But lumber has been shrinking for years. The amount of dressing it takes to smooth a plank has increased to the point that mills produce boards with up to 25 percent of their nominal size missing. Most 1-inch boards emerge at ¾; 2-inch material often dresses out at 1½.

Unfortunately, an inconsistency between the name and the size is not the end of it: even pieces called the same size are different. The rougher grades of 2-inch pine, fir and spruce arrive from the lumberyard at a fairly consistent 1¾. The better grades of 2-inch pine, however, measure closer to 1⅞. Pine labelled ¾-inch (1¼ inches) measures anywhere from 1 inch to 1⅛ inches depending on what day it is, and the thickness of 1-inch cedar at local yards varies even more.

In part, the variety of sizes has to do with who is doing the cutting. A local mill north of my hometown is particularly generous, consistently trimming out hefty chunks of wood like the bread maker who tosses in an extra bun to make a baker's dozen. Larger outfits, however, don't toss in anything, presumably on the understandable theory that if they save 1/16 inch on every cut, then for every 12 "one inch" boards they cut, they get one free.

Even if everyone in the world cut to exactly the same specifications, humidity and the care with which the wood is dried and subsequently stored would alter its precise size by the time it got to you. As lumber dries, it shrinks, plain and simple. In order to ensure dimensional stability, serious cabinetmakers dry all their own materials and keep on hand a well-used moisture meter, which measures the water content of a plank by checking how well it conducts an electrical current. They don't work with wood until all the pieces they need have reached the same moisture level.

This book, however, assumes that you do not dry and store your own wood, that you do not own a thickness planer with which to create perfectly uniform materials and that you are therefore, to some extent, at the mercy of the lumberyard and day-to-day fluctuations in the relative humidity. For that reason, many of the instructions for these projects discourage measuring and cutting everything at once and assembling the finished pieces. Instead, it is recommended that you measure and cut as you go. Skip the tape measure and the arithmetic whenever possible in favour of holding your workpiece in its intended spot and marking it directly. That way, if the 2-inch material you use for a project's legs is 1/16 inch smaller than usual, you won't get caught with a gap between the legs that is a full ⅛ inch bigger than assumed by the plans.

you use will move around and shrink and try to twist and warp and bow and cup. In general, this book encourages you to be aware of the humidity level in your shop and suggests some commonsense steps to limit its effects.

In order to simplify matters and to encourage you to make the kinds of modifications that are suggested or implied in the instructions, each project is accompanied by a blank sheet of graph paper. It is not just for decoration. You can use the page to work out any changes necessary to tailor the piece to your particular needs and keep it as a permanent record for future reference.

If under your hands, any of these projects evolve into an interesting new form or if you develop a clever construction technique—even, heaven forbid, should you unmask a blunder in the instructions—draw it on these pages so that anyone else using your copy of the book will benefit. And let me know. Perhaps I can include your contribution in future printings.

Most how-to books assume that readers have a lot of money and no brains. The earnest author, conscious of his or her potential legal liability, carefully warns the backyard builder to don protective glasses before approaching the workbench but assumes in the next paragraph that the reader not only owns a dovetail router jig or a compound mitre saw but also knows how to use it.

By deliberate contrast, I assume that the readers of this book will know enough to protect their eyes and to employ the safety equipment that accompanies power tools—that they will, for example, keep scarves and loose clothing away from spinning machinery without being reminded on these pages. Having said that, I also assume that most backyard builders do not actually own much spinning machinery and—by preference or necessity—rely mainly on basic hand tools.

The projects included in this book can all be completed with the following tools:

## HAMMER
You can pay any price for a hammer, and if you own a $3 special purchased from a bin of factory seconds, this is your excuse to go out and buy something better. A good hammer does not hit your fingers nearly as often as a cheap one does and provides the kind of control necessary to avoid surrounding every nailhead you sink with a series of half-moon hammer divots. For building furniture, you want a finishing hammer that weighs 16 ounces or so.

## SCREWDRIVERS
Because of some mysterious national fastener chauvinism, most Americans have to make do without the benefit of infinitely superior Canadian Robertson screws. The back pages of magazines such as *Fine Homebuilding* advertise "square-head screws for reduced cam-out," but they have to be ordered from a specialty store, so there isn't much need in the American shop for the good old Red Robby, the red-handled #2 Robertson screwdriver. It is, however, the standard driver necessary for all the wood screws referred to in this book. Numbers 6, 8 and 10 screws all come with the same-sized

socket. In areas where Robertsons are unavailable, you will need a #2 Phillips screwdriver or driver bit for your drill.

## CHISELS
Buy a set of chisels if you do not already own one. Having the correct size for the job sometimes makes a noticeable difference in the end product and always makes you feel better. Just as important as owning the chisels is knowing how to sharpen them. If you do not own a good stone, buy one of those too, and teach yourself how to put a mirror finish on the cutting face. Also learn how to stroke a fine micro-bevel onto the cutting edge. A chisel that works well should be able to shave the hair from your arm; it should also be able to pass the rather safer test of slicing a paper-thin curl from the end grain of a softwood board.

## HANDSAWS
You need a good crosscut saw for sizing planks. For building outdoor furniture, strike a compromise between the rough cutting speed of a 7-tooth-per-inch saw and the fine delicacy of a 12-tooth-per-inch finish saw. Something around a 9-point will serve you well; that is the saw used by traditional carpenters for doing outside trim. You also need a backsaw (so named for the solid metal spine that reinforces the blade) for finish cuts and for use with your mitre box.

## MITRE BOX
For at least one project in this book, you will have to have a mitre box. For other projects, the 45-degree cuts you need can be done with careful marking and a hand-held saw or with a speed square and a circular saw. Buy the best mitre box you can afford—watch for them in garage sales. One that comes with its own saw and an adjustable metal guide is best.

## COPING SAW, BOW SAW OR JIGSAW
A couple of the projects in this book require cutting curves into structural members or on the finished surface of a table. To cut a curve, you need a saw that can make it around a corner. If you own a coping saw, you can use it for the cuts you will need, although the fine teeth

of most coping blades will make it slow going. Alternatively, you can use a bow saw, an old-fashioned-looking instrument that seems to be reappearing in tool stores. These usually hold a variety of blades, and you can select one with bigger teeth for cutting 2-inch material. Or, if you own a selection of power tools, you probably already have a jigsaw. Even an inexpensive version will handle the limited demands of the projects contained in this book.

## CIRCULAR SAW

A cheap circular saw is a menace to your fingers and should be thrown away before it is too late. A good-quality circular saw sells for a couple of hundred dollars at a tool centre and should be used for those jobs that aren't as easy to do by hand. The saw should have a solid foot or base and a fence guide that attaches firmly for those times when you want to rip lumber or trim the edge of a piece of plywood. Your circular saw needs plenty of power (13 amps) and a good firm spring on the blade guard. Many affordable saws are now equipped with a power brake, which is worth having.

There are dozens of saw blades available, many of them designed for specific applications. For building outdoor furniture, you need a combination blade with lots of carbide teeth. More teeth means a cleaner cut; carbide means a longer life for the blade. For cutting plywood, use a plywood blade to avoid excessive tearing. And don't use your furniture-making blade when you take on a weekend renovation project that involves burning through old plaster and nails.

Here's one of those knee-jerk warnings: Always unplug your saw when changing blades or setting the depth of the shoe or setting the fence or measuring the distance from the blade to the edge of the base. After blades and the brushes in the motor, which need to be replaced now and then, the plug should be the first thing to wear out.

## ELECTRIC DRILL

A cheap drill will not hurt you the way a cheap circular saw might, but a good variable-speed drill will do more than make holes—it will also do a fine, gentle job of driving home screws. You

## COMBINATION SQUARE

*Everyone who owns a combination square already knows about using it to mark 90-degree and 45-degree lines across a workpiece. It is also a good ruler to use for any other marking and layout tasks. As well, the housing that slides up and down on the metal rule almost always contains a tiny spirit level, and good squares always include a miniature scratch awl, which many people do not even know they have. Look closely at yours. If you find a small knob resembling the winding wheel on a watch, that is the head of the awl. Pull it out.*

*If you have ever purchased a used combination square from someone who knew his or her way around a shop, you may have found a notch filed in one end of the steel rule itself. That notch is for one of the handier uses of your square, because with it and a pencil, you can strike a line perfectly parallel to the straightedge of any board or sheet of plywood. Just set the distance that you want the line to fall from the edge, then with the pencil point set in the notch and held on the work surface, slide the lip of the square along the edge of the wood. The same technique also allows you to reproduce a particular measurement over and over again. If, for instance, you want to mark the position of screws at the ends of each of several tabletop boards, set the square to the distance that you want the screws to be from the ends, and then mark each separate board in turn.*

cannot get along without hand-held screwdrivers, but even if you have forearms like Popeye, a bit chucked in a drill will earn your gratitude time after time. It is also helpful if your drill is reversible for those occasions when you install all the screws before you remember the glue.

## TABLE SAW

In many of the projects included in this book, a table saw can be used to speed things up or simplify some of the steps involved; in a few instances, the instructions mention specific table-saw techniques. With the exception of the tray-and-stand ensemble described on pages 112-

116, however, all of these projects can be completed with hand tools. Even for the tray and stand, a determined craftsperson could cut the required materials from rough hardwood stock using a ripsaw and a set of planes. (It should be noted, however, that a person with that worthy brand of 19th-century patience probably knows more about building furniture than anyone associated with this book. And also probably owns a table saw.)

## BLOCK PLANE

A block plane is a remarkably versatile tool: Treat its cutting edge with the same careful attention that you lavish on your chisels, and reach for it first every time you have trouble fitting two pieces of wood together. The blade should be sharp enough to shave end grain, the handle should fit in your palm, and if you have adjusted it properly, it should work with the same satisfying perfection that you feel when you hit a tennis ball with the sweet spot of a racquet.

## SANDERS

The better the sander, the less effort you will have to make when you use it. For these projects, you will need a belt sander and a palm sander. A larger orbital sander for the tabletops will do a quicker job but isn't necessary.

## DOZUKI

The dozuki, or Japanese pull saw, is perhaps a luxury, but it's one that will earn its keep in your shop. The dozuki differs from Western saws in the way its teeth are sharpened and set and therefore in the way it clears sawdust with each stroke. As well, instead of cutting as you push, it bites in on the pull of your stroke. If you've ever heard the expression "you can't push a rope" and had a day when that seems to apply to the way your fine finishing saw is binding in a cut, then you understand the advantages of the way a dozuki does its job. Its ultrafine blade means almost no saw kerf, and you simply replace the blades when they get dull. A dozuki can take the place of a backsaw for many chores.

## SCRATCH AWL

The scratch awl does several things well. It nestles perfectly in the palm of your hand. It has a sweet-feeling heft and balance. It looks wonderful, albeit slightly menacing. And it is handy to have around for marking lines and for starting holes for small screws and finishing nails. Keep the tip sharp by touching it up with a fine file now and then, and use the awl instead of a pencil. Well, think about it anyway, because even if you don't actually strike all your lines with sharpened steel, understanding the reasons for doing so will encourage you to keep your pencil tuned up and to use it correctly.

## NAIL SETS

Nail sets come in a variety of sizes and are used to drive the heads of nails below the surface of the wood. You need one small enough for finishing nails and another large enough for banging home 2½-inch ardox nails.

## UTILITY KNIFE

For shop work, buy a utility knife with an indestructible metal handle that does not allow the blade to retract; it makes a firmer cut and lasts longer as well. The insides never fall out when you are in a hurry for a new blade, and you don't need the blade to be hidden away, since you won't be stashing the knife in your work pouch all day long.

## PENCILS

Keep lots of pencils in your shop, and try not to fall into the habit of leaving one tucked behind your ear when you stop work for the day, or you'll wind up having a lot of pencils in your house instead. Installing a pencil sharpener in the shop or near the back door is a great idea, but few people are that organized.

## TAPE MEASURE

For work in the shop, you rarely need a tape longer than 12 feet (you don't actually need a tape of any length nearly as often as most people think). Buy one that locks in place firmly and feels good in your hand.

## DRILL BITS

Unless you are using them in a drill press, good (expensive) bits in the small sizes tend to break just as easily as the cheap ones. If you are using the larger sizes only for occasional drilling in softwoods, then cheap ones will do for that too. Buy one of those handy boxed sets rather than trying to figure out which particular bits you need job by job.

## PUTTY KNIFE

Putty knives are inexpensive, which is probably why they seem to disappear practically every time you use one. Since they always show up later, the trick is to buy a different size to replace each lost knife. Over time, you will accumulate a full set, which looks impressive but is not essential.

## WRENCHES AND SOCKET SETS

If you own a socket set, you probably have everything you need for the projects contained in this book. A pair of medium-sized adjustable wrenches will also do just fine.

## CLAMPS

Become a scrounger and collector of clamps. (See "Clamps," page 116.)

## THE LARGEST TOOLS

There are whole books written on the theory and history of workbenches, and unlike many subjects about which whole books are written, there really is a lifetime's worth of stuff to say about benches. The basics, however, are that the bench should be about 30 inches high but should suit your height, the state of your lower back and the kind of work you do most often. If, for example, you spend a lot of time bending slightly so that you can get your weight be-hind a chisel, you might want a lower bench. A bench doesn't need immensely strong legs unless you plan to rebuild your car engine on it (in which case you're going to need another, cleaner bench for woodwork anyway). The work surface has to be able to withstand hammering and chiselling, but more important than great strength is stability, which can be achieved by anchoring the bench top to at least one wall with some right-angle brackets and good long screws. That way, when you clamp a workpiece to the bench top, the whole thing won't shift as you start planing or chiselling.

The bench top itself should be substantial enough to absorb all the banging you need to do. You don't want any bounce or give at all—no hopping or rebounding or leaping or skipping. You can build such a surface from layers of heavy plywood laminated together to produce something 1½ to 2 inches thick. Or you can assemble 2x4s on edge and plane them to a uniform flatness. But the easiest thing to do is visit the local wrecker and buy a used solid-core door. In my city, every time they renovate or demolish an institutional building, a whole pile of workbench tops ends up at my favourite junkyard. Remove the lock-set assembly, and fill the hole with a hunk of wood.

You also need a section of floor that you know is perfectly flat so that you can do your final assembly on it. Despite what you might think, the last thing in the world you should trust for flatness is a concrete floor. Check it first with something absolutely straight, such as the factory edge of a piece of plywood.

The action of the elements on wooden furniture is inevitable—and inevitably unkind. Rain soaks into the wood, where it supports rot. Sunshine dries the wood, opening joints and cracking boards. Ultraviolet rays break down the wood fibres. Given all that finishes must accomplish, it is worth applying them correctly. Here are some suggestions.

## LATEX VERSUS ALKYD

If you have spent any time in a paint store over the past several years, you have seen the tide turn against oil-based paints and stains. The shelf space devoted to oils (also called alkyds) has dwindled, and the options available in water-based alternatives have taken up all the slack and more. The reasons are obvious.

Cleanup after working with latex finishes requires only soap and water. By contrast, alkyd products require special solvents, and washing up after painting a table and some chairs with an oil paint can take more time than you spent applying the finish to the wood.

Alkyd paints and the solvents required to work with them contribute greenhouse gases and also take their toll on people inhaling the fumes. I know someone who passed out while working with oil paint. I have never heard of anyone being felled by acrylic latex.

Some alkyd products still contain linseed oil as a basic ingredient, so in order to combat the mildew that feeds on the oil itself, those finishes also contain powerful antifungal poisons.

Every finish available in alkyds can now be found in latex paints, including the high gloss you may want for a tabletop, and after a curing period of 30 to 60 days, latex paints can be washed as vigorously and as often as oils. Oil-based stains, traditionally valued for their durability, have large labels advertising a 3-year warranty. The water-based stains have smaller print—and 12-year warranties.

Yet even as water-based finishes gain the upper hand, professionals continue to praise the traditional oil-based finishes, claiming they last longer, give better protection and cover in fewer coats while yielding a better finish. Some of this may be a matter of old habits dying hard, but it can't be dismissed out of hand.

Every professional and paint-store service person I asked praised the latex products to the sky, then admitted that for their own lawn furniture, they would use an oil product. With a couple of exceptions, however, they all added one important caveat. If there is any doubt about the moisture content of the wood, go with latex. In addition to being easier to apply and clean up, latex works far better over less-than-perfectly-dry wood. Moisture breathes back out through latex without lifting the paint.

## PAINTS AND STAINS AND VARNISH AND LINSEED OIL

No matter what you do to finish a piece of outdoor furniture, you will have to do it again someday. Keep that in mind as you decide whether to stain or paint or oil or wax the chair or table you've completed. Of all the woods readily available in North American lumberyards, only cedar takes care of itself if left exposed to the elements. (Cypress no longer falls within the category of readily available, nor does white oak.)

The naturally weather-resistant woods contain their own herbicides, fungicides and pesticides, but for all the others, you have to either provide the poisons and weather sealant or accept that they will rot in the coming years. There are places where unprotected wooden objects last, but they are the arid exceptions. Everywhere else, dampness creates an environment for wood decay.

Paints and stains do two things: they form a seal around the wood to prevent moisture from getting to the fibres, in effect shrink-wrapping it; and they coat the surface of the wood with various preservatives that kill organisms responsible for the breakdown of wood under natural conditions. Different paints and stains do these things to varying degrees. On one end of the scale, preservative stains take the toxic route. On the other end, heavy opaque paints tend to rely on sealing the wood and protecting it from the ultraviolet rays of the sun, another force that breaks down the seal between the coating and the wood beneath. If you use varnish, be sure to purchase a "spar" varnish, one containing a UV block.

Even with built-in sunscreen, varnishes and most paints eventually wear and lift away from the wood. To re-cover your furniture, you will first have to remove the old finish down to the bare wood. Stains, by contrast, just fade gently away, and a new coating usually soaks into weatherworn wood faster than the first coat did when the wood was new.

Like lots of people, you may think of linseed oil as a fine old-fashioned way to protect wood. If so, there are a couple of things you should know. Boiled linseed oil contains a drying agent that causes it to harden. Raw linseed oil does not contain any such additive and is not intended as a protective finish for anything, although it makes leather nice and supple. In either form, linseed oil is a medium for fungi and will sustain lovely blooms of mould under the right conditions. It is not really the thing for outdoor furniture.

Finally, do not use opaque or semiopaque stains on such surfaces as chairs and benches that people rub against. The colour will not wear right off the wood, but it can leave a light tint on clothes.

## PAINTING TIPS

Pay attention to instructions about the proper conditions for applying the finish you choose. Painting on a hot day in direct sunlight can result in blisters forming under the finish. Painting with alkyd resins in the evening, especially after days of high humidity, can flatten the paint, causing dull splotches on what is supposed to be a glossy finish. The moisture from the damp evening air can also lead to blistering, and for the same reason, do not apply an alkyd product unless the lumber is completely dry. If you seal moisture inside a layer of dried alkyd paint, the first hot day will cause it to expand, blowing the paint up like bubblegum.

The purpose of undercoats is to seal the surface and to provide a uniform texture. If you plan to use an oil-based finish on new wood, where all surfaces are the same, you will do well to thin the paint by 15 to 20 percent with varsol for greater penetration, then apply a finish coat over that.

Allow each coat of alkyd finish to dry completely before adding another coat; otherwise,

## SHELLAC

*You should use shellac occasionally if only because it's the most interesting finish in your shop. Manufacturers still refine it from "lac," a secretion the female Asian lac beetle uses for nest-building. Workers still harvest lac by snapping twigs from trees where the beetles have eaten the bark and built their fortified homes. Although lac has been around for 3,000 years, the market for shellac continues to grow at a rate of 5 percent every year, and covering knots is about the least exciting thing it does. It's the finish on pianos and an edible coating for pharmaceutical products, candies and fruit. There is even a little shellac on cornflakes to keep them crunchy.*

*If you plan to paint a finished piece of furniture instead of staining it, first locate all the knots and mop up any leaking resin using a rag soaked in mineral spirits. Then cover all the knots completely with shellac before applying the first coat of paint. Use a pigmented stain-hiding shellac, because it seals the resins behind a nonpermeable film and also hides the darkness of the knot, allowing you to get complete coverage with fewer coats of paint. If you forget to prepare your surfaces with shellac, the resin will drain from the knots for years to come, bleeding not only through the first primer coat and finish coat but also through successive attempts to cover them.*

*If you do shellac the knots—on the seat and arms of a chair, for example—you should then apply an oil-based paint. The physical properties of fully dried alkyd paint resemble those of the shellac, so the two materials work well together. The softer latex paints, however, do not typically react to changes in temperature and humidity at the same rate as the hard shellac coating. With the two materials expanding and contracting at different rates, the wear and tear of daily use takes a greater toll. On the other hand, if you shellac knots on the legs of a table or other low-traffic surface, feel free to apply a latex primer and finish coat. Be certain, however, that the label on the shellac specifically states that it is compatible with waterborne finishes: some shellacs contain wax, and wax and water don't mix.*

it will take forever for that next coat to set.

Do not apply most brands of latex paint over an alkyd primer. If you do, you will be able to scrape the finish off with a fingernail. You can apply alkyd paints over a latex undercoat, because the oil base will penetrate the latex layer. Most latex paints, however, cannot soak through dried oil paint to lock onto the surface below.

Even though you can apply alkyd over latex, avoid doing so, because oil paints dry harder than latex. Furniture gets banged and handled and sat upon, and under such heavy-wear conditions, the top coat should not be harder than the layer supporting it. To understand the problem with hard coatings over soft, imagine applying a brittle layer of glossy paint to a piece of foam rubber and think of what would happen the first time you sat on it. For the same reason, don't put hard-finish floor paints over any other paints. Floor paints might seem like a good idea for your outdoor furniture, but they often use an entirely different chemical process than do standard alkyds and latex. In addition, they are almost always self-priming, which means you apply them directly onto bare wood. Unless you have been given careful assurances to the contrary, avoid floor paints for outdoor furniture anyway. A brittle finish does not stick well in corners or nooks or crannies, and unless you anticipate regular dancing on the tabletops, the scuff resistance of floor paints won't be an advantage.

## PREPARATION

Before you begin, make sure all surfaces are free of sanding dust and everything else, including wax and grease and dribbles of whatever you ate when you sat down at your almost-finished table for lunch.

If there are dark mildew blooms on the wood, get rid of them before painting or staining. If they will not sand out, wash them off or, rather, scrub them off with a dilute solution of bleach. You can purchase commercial mildew washes, but you'll find that nothing works better than chlorine bleach. Alternatively, you can purchase a paint designed for high coverage, but if the label does not specifically claim to hide mildew, do not apply it to affected wood. Some

paints contain bases that actually provide food for the mildew, and the stain grows straight through in a big hurry.

Even if the lumber you used looks so smooth that you cannot bear to sand it, go over it lightly to give a little texture to the surface. That lovely polished sheen on some boards is called "mill glaze" and comes from the sharp knives of high-speed planers. Paint doesn't stick to mill glaze.

If you are painting rather than staining, paint all countersunk holes before applying the wood filler, then precoat all dried wood filler and let that paint dry before you apply a final overall coat. Fillers usually absorb finishes with a greater thirst than the surrounding surface and will produce rough spots on the paint unless you seal them first.

Bear in mind that the supersmooth finish desirable for indoor furniture is not necessarily the best thing for outdoor pieces. While you want to remove all the rough spots and the raised grain that follows the application of a primer coat, a slightly rougher surface provides an infinity of tiny grooves for the paint or stain to key into, helping it get a grip on the surface. In other words, you don't need to use sandpaper finer than 100 grit. To understand this point, remember that paint does not stick to glass nearly as well as it sticks to your wool sweater. If you want to apply a light stain, however, you're better to get things as smooth as possible so that the pigment in the stain does not highlight every sanding mark you've made.

## PAINTING DISCLAIMER

When it comes time to finish your furniture, ignore most of the things you know, even if you learned them in this book, and ask careful questions on the day you go to purchase your paint. There are many eternal verities in the world of woodworking, but none of them has anything to do with paints and stains. Everything changes, and under pressure from consumers who want more environmentally responsible products, manufacturers continue to create new alternatives almost monthly. During the week I worked on the painting recommendations for this book, I used a latex semigloss bathroom paint that, contrary to all accepted wisdom, instructed me to apply an alkyd primer. There are new oil-based paints that wash up in soap and water, which seems like a contradiction in terms, and decorating stores now sell clear and semitransparent nonstain, nonvarnish, nonpaint "coatings." These come as a system designed primarily for natural-finish exterior-wood siding. The hardness of these coating systems suggests that they would also work well on outdoor furniture, but do a bit of research before you buy.

Always ask your retailer, and read instructions and any product-specification sheets available where you buy your paints and other coatings.

A bicycle rack does not count as outdoor furniture; yard hardware, maybe. But the design history of this particular rack illustrates the happenstance evolution of a building project so nicely that it belongs in this book. If you examine a problem, a solution appears, and if you keep looking at a problem long enough, a *simpler* solution appears.

My friend Steve and I, with a shop full of tools, years of experience, a healthy scrap pile to work with and a whole afternoon to kill, decided to solve the problem of too many bicycles in my backyard. As a starting point, we had the example of every bicycle rack we had ever seen, and perhaps we got off on the wrong foot by picturing the steel upright versions found in most schoolyards, the ones that look like a small section of fence with vertical slats for the front wheels to slide through. By the time we were finished our design plan, we had created something about as straightforward as a letter opener, but in the process, we had invented a veritable Rube Goldberg machine. We were at first humbled, you might say, by our own assumptions. We succeeded, however, by sticking with our determination that there had to be a simpler way.

A large bicycle wheel has a diameter of 26 inches; the hub is therefore 13 inches off the ground. That seemed relevant, and we took it as an initial consideration. We were also pretty clear that all we needed was support for one of the two wheels. And we wanted something sturdy and aesthetically pleasing—a suitable testament to our combined wit and engineering prowess.

Then we started in. The empty stretch of wall by the back door seemed a natural place to locate a rack, so I imagined setting a 2x4 some distance out from the foundation and then nailing four pairs of 2x2s on an angle from there up to the wall. The bicycle wheels would slip between each pair and be held upright.

We decided that nailing each 2x2 directly into the wall would probably not produce the strongest or cleanest-looking arrangement, so perhaps the 2x2s should be attached to a crosspiece which could be fixed to the wall with something sturdy like carriage bolts. This, of course, raised the question of whether the battens on the board-and-batten wall would have to be cut so that the crosspiece could be set flush to the wall or whether it could just rest on top of the battens. But we set aside that problem for the time being.

While I worried that the design would leave the lower support sitting loosely on the ground, Steve pointed out that there would also be only two points of contact for each wheel. The bottom of each wheel would be free to move, and the bikes could topple over, which would bend the spokes. To address both these problems, we amended our sketch, adding a brace that extended out from the base of the wall to anchor each end of the lower 2x4 and four more pairs of 2x2s that reached back to the wall at ground level from each of the four existing pairs. All of these additional pieces then required another 2x4 to which they could be attached, and that piece, too, had to be anchored to the wall.

Already things seemed out of hand. We needed carriage bolts and holes drilled in the wall. We needed three longitudinal braces and a total of 16 2x2s, half of them cut on a careful angle at each end. As well, there was some concern about whether the bikes would fit inside the frame and whether the wheel would roll past the bottom 2x4 before the front forks banged into the sloping 2x2s. We were going to have to level everything during installation, and it occurred to me that since the wall is concrete at ground level, we were going to have to find either concrete nails or Tapcon screws on a Sunday afternoon.

Next, we imagined carving little slots in the outside bottom brace and perhaps notching each of the diagonals so that the hub of the wheels would fit. Then we worried about the extent to which this would weaken everything.

We discussed the possibility of metal U-shaped frames mounted in pairs on the wall so that the front tire could be slipped in between for support, but since our materials were limited to the wood in the shop, we gave that up. And we talked about a frame from which the bikes could be hung on hooks.

Finally, we found ourselves wondering out loud whether or not we had a whole afternoon to kill after all. And then we gave up.

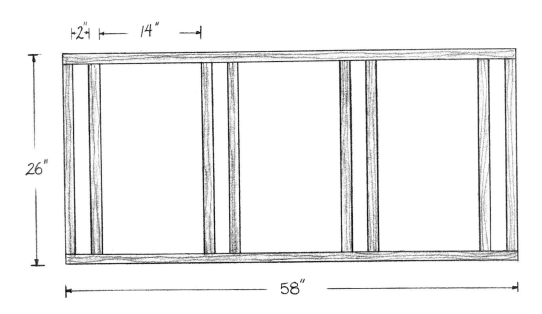

As we prepared to leave the shop, I commented that it was too bad we couldn't build something like a ladder with pairs of 2x2s in place of the rungs and somehow attach that a little way out from the wall.

And then we realized that if we used something wider than 2x2s, the whole thing wouldn't need to be set away from the wall at all and would still provide enough support. That left us with the plan shown above, which is too basic to describe clearly in words.

This bike rack can be made of either cedar or pressure-treated wood using 1x6 or ¾x6 for a bit more stability, and since it will be in contact with the ground, it should be coated with a preservative. It can be assembled with either 2½-inch nails or wood screws. Beyond that, I don't think any instructions are necessary. Measure the width of the tires on your bicycles;

if they are mountain bikes, the tires will be just over 2 inches wide. These plans keep the rack as small as possible and require bikes to be alternated, with the first having its front wheel in the rack and the next the rear wheel so that handlebars don't get tangled. If you have lots of room, increase the distance between the wheel slots to 25 inches or more, and all bikes can then be placed front wheel first.

Postscript: I discovered that once it was assembled and in use, this rack works in either the horizontal or the upright position. The day after our design triumph, while I was still thinking I should patent our invention, I saw a rack just like it sitting in a playground, which illustrates another law of design: If you've been wrestling with a problem and hoping for a solution, look around you—someone has probably already come up with it.

### WOOD SCREWS

Everyone knows what a wood screw is, and almost everyone knows that they come in various lengths. Some people are not aware, however, that each of the various lengths also comes in a variety of thicknesses and that the wrong-diameter screw can create an impressive amount of frustration. When you buy screws, check the length; if you screw a 2x2 to another 2x2 using something 3½ inches long, it will come right through and then some. But also check the diameter, because if you drive a 2½-inch #12 wood screw through one 2x2 and into another, you will likely split them both.

The numbering system is straightforward: the higher the number, the thicker the screw. The sizes you'll find in most hardware and lumber-supply stores range from #4 to #12. For almost all applications described in this book, you can use #8 screws. The exceptions are noted.

Drill pilot holes for all screws. You will never create a problem by predrilling, but you will often avoid one.

If you can afford them, use brass screws. Because they don't rust, they don't require any protection or concern. Always drill pilot holes for brass screws, whether you are driving into hardwood or softwood. Without a pilot hole, the soft brass will break off in the wood and/or the screwdriver bit will strip the socket on the head of the screw, both of which are extremely annoying problems.

### NAILS

In some of the projects described in this book, you have the option of using nails instead of screws. Presumably if you opt for this quicker expedient, you will not be planning to countersink and plug the nail holes, so in order to avoid rust stains, you should use galvanized nails. To drive those nails, don't use a framing hammer—the one with the waffled striking face—because it will tear away the protective coating. Use ardox nails because they have a greater grip.

If while you are driving a nail into a softwood such as spruce or pine, you miss your swing and create one of those crescent moons, immediately spit on the dent. The moisture will sometimes—though not always—reinflate the crushed wood cells and erase the mark. For the more delicate craftsperson who works in a shop equipped with a sink, a dampened cloth will do just as well.

Keep an assortment of finishing nails on hand, from ½-inch to 3- or 4-inch. Although they are not adequate fasteners for the kinds of projects described in this book, finishing nails can be extremely handy to tack things together while you wait for glue to dry or to hold two pieces in place while you drill holes for bolts.

### BOLTS

In situations that require more clamping strength than wood screws or nails can provide or in situations where the everyday use of the furniture will work on the joints and tend to loosen them, a bolt may be necessary. In most cases, a carriage bolt provides the most elegant finished appearance, because all that shows of the head is a rounded dome. Carriage bolts are also handy because they have a squared-off lip just below the head that binds in the wood and prevents the bolt from turning as you tighten the nut. If you prefer a different look or if you cannot find carriage bolts in the size you need, you can use hex bolts.

Use washers on the nut end of a carriage bolt and on both ends of a hex bolt. The washers prevent the bolt head or the nut from sinking into the wood, which is important if you ever want to be able to get a wrench back in place to loosen things up again.

If you use hex bolts, then instead of nuts and washers, you can use so-called palnuts, or T-nuts, as they are now sometimes called. A T-nut is a small threaded cylinder topped by a collar in such a way that the whole thing viewed from the side looks like the letter T. These give hex bolts the same one-handed convenience as carriage bolts, because small teeth project from the collar, and as the bolt tightens, the teeth bite into the wood to prevent the nut from turning. With everything snugged down, the nut sits flush with the wood, and if you buy the correct length of bolt (or if you own a hacksaw), the bolt does not need to project at all.

Most important of all, keep lots of screws and nails and bolts on hand. Do not figure out exactly how many you need and then buy just those. All you have to do is miscalculate once and go through the gas-burning, time-wasting, aplomb-consuming inconvenience of going all the way back to the lumberyard for two screws to cancel out a lifetime's worth of saving your money one wood screw at a time. (This advice, of course, does not apply to brass fasteners. They cost more than gasoline, and with prices as high as $5 for each 4-inch brass carriage bolt, counting is worth it.)

## CUTTING DIAGRAM AND MATERIALS LIST

## MATERIALS LIST

one 10-foot ⁵⁄₄x6
two 8-foot ⁵⁄₄x6s

2½" galvanized ardox nails

## PARTS LIST

2 side pieces                     ⁵⁄₄x6x58"
8 crosspieces                     ⁵⁄₄x6x24"

## CUTTING DIAGRAM

10-foot ⁵⁄₄x6

| SIDE PIECE | SIDE PIECE | |
|------------|------------|---|

8-foot ⁵⁄₄x6

| CROSSPIECE | CROSSPIECE | CROSSPIECE | CROSSPIECE |
|------------|------------|------------|------------|

8-foot ⁵⁄₄x6

| CROSSPIECE | CROSSPIECE | CROSSPIECE | CROSSPIECE |
|------------|------------|------------|------------|

Benches are for sitting on, standing on, putting things down on, building forts with and hiding behind. Weekend home renovators usually use the nearest bench instead of the perfectly good sawhorses in the shed at the back of the yard, which is why my benches are all decorated with splatters of every paint that goes on our storm windows and trim. Benches don't get a whole lot of respect, but they usually get a good deal of use and, if you count every moment of relief that follows the realization that your bench is just the solution to some unlikely problem, a fair bit of affection. Given all they are asked to do, then, benches need to be strong.

Like a small trestle table, this bench consists of two upright legs, each of which includes a crosspiece at the bottom to provide a wide stance on the ground and a crosspiece to hold the top.

I designed my version of a trestle bench to use up various sizes of scrap left over from building a deck; the dimensions of the bench followed from the material at hand. The finished piece proved so solid and pleasing to look at, however, that I present it here exactly as it first evolved. Since it requires short pieces of 4x4, 2x4, 2x6 and 2x8, you might want to go scrounging in your own scraps or in the off-cut pile of a construction site for your materials. Either that, or plan to build more than one to make the purchase of materials worthwhile.

Assembly is perfectly straightforward once notches are cut in the 4x4 uprights. In the original, I used 2½-inch galvanized ardox nails to fasten everything together, but #8 wood screws

of the same length are appropriate. The notches should be as long as a 2x6 is wide and as deep as a 2x6 is thick.

1 Cut everything to length, and then cut tapers on the arms and feet. Mark the centre of the crosspieces, and mark the centre of the notched legs as well so that you can line everything up. Spread a waterproof glue on the inside of the notch, then fasten the crosspieces with screws placed in the familiar "5" pattern found on dice. Check that the bottom of the feet and the tops of the arms are at 90 degrees to the 4x4 and therefore parallel to one another.

2 When the glue has set, place the legs upright, and fasten the top members in place. The tops should overhang the arms by 3 inches on each end and half an inch on the sides. You do not have to use a 2x8 and two 2x4s for the top, but a wide board in the middle will cover the end grain of the 4x4 and protect it from water. If your scrap pile contains chunks of 2x6s, three of them will do instead. The finished top will be about an inch wider, which you can either live with or trim. Spread more glue, and nail or screw each of the top boards to the crosspieces with two fasteners at each end of the 2x4s and three at each end of the 2x8. Drive two fasteners down through the middle board and into the top of each 4x4. The fasteners in the 4x4 will stabilize the bench in the same way as would a small triangular brace fixed into the 90-degree junction of the leg and the top; that is, the bench will be much more resistant to racking (collapsing sideways).

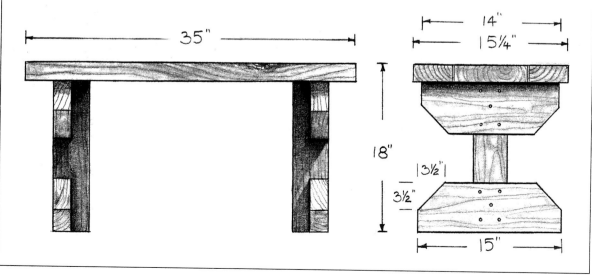

All three bench plans call for notches to be cut into the legs. In one case, notches in the 4x4 leg accept the 2x6 crosspieces that form the feet at the bottom and arms to support the top. In another, the notches accept skirts that fit under the top piece and stretch the length of the bench to brace the legs at either end. And in the third case, a brace extends through notches in the legs to provide additional support.

To make notches, begin by marking the area to be cut away. Take your measurements directly from the piece that will be fitting into the notch. In other words, do not assume that lumber from the yard is any precise dimension. It is best to hold the crosspiece or skirt in place and mark directly onto the leg, ignoring the numeric measurements completely.

You can cut the notch by carefully marking all lines onto the workpiece and using a hand-held crosscut saw or ripsaw, but if you have limited experience with the ripsaw, practise first on a piece of scrap. Alternatively, if you own a circular saw and have some experience wielding it, you can hog out the notch using the power tool to make a series of cuts ⅛ inch apart and then clean up with a chisel.

To use the circular-saw method, clamp the leg pieces together; that way, you get identical results at both ends of your bench. As well, the larger surface you get by clamping several pieces on edge will be easier to

work on with the hand-held power saw, and by doing them all at once, you will be done faster. Of course, if you make a mistake, you'll be in two or four times as much trouble, so instead of "measure twice, cut once," you may want to measure four times—or eight.

Set the saw blade to the depth you require or even a little shy of it, and once again, rather than using a tape measure to transfer the measurement, hold the (unplugged) circular saw against the workpiece and set the blade to the line you've marked. As you make the first cut, guide the foot of the circular saw with a square (See "Crosscuts With the Rafter Square," page 81) to ensure that the cut at the edge of the notch runs straight, then make as many additional cuts as you can through the wood you want to remove.

Break out the remaining sections of wood—they'll snap away like a set of fragile dominoes—and clean up the surface with a chisel.

When using this technique, be careful to keep the saw level as it exits the far side of the wood you are cutting. The weight of the saw itself and the pressure of your hand pushing it will make the saw tend to tip forward once the front edge of the base reaches beyond the work area. When that happens, the blade will cut more deeply than you want it to. Keep the saw flat by ensuring that the rear of the base remains in contact with the work surface.

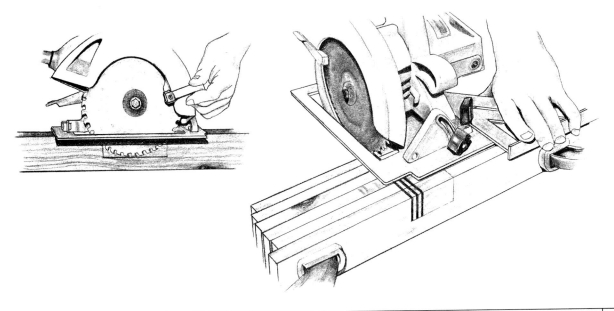

# CUTTING DIAGRAM AND MATERIALS LIST

## MATERIALS LIST (for two benches)

one 6-foot 4x4
one 10-foot 2x6
two 6-foot 2x4s
one 6-foot 2x8

2½" #8 wood screws
   or 2½" galvanized ardox nails
waterproof glue

## PARTS LIST (for one bench)

| | | |
|---|---|---|
| 2 legs | | 4x4x16" |
| 2 arms | | 2x6x14" |
| 2 feet | | 2x6x15" |
| 2 top pieces | | 2x4x35" |
| 1 top piece | | 2x8x35" |

## CUTTING DIAGRAM

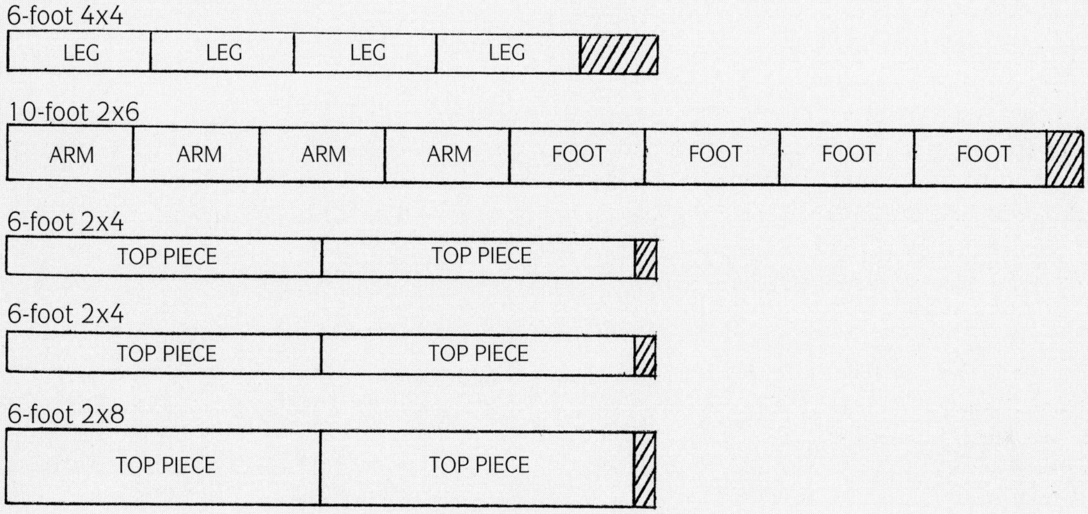

6-foot 4x4

| LEG | LEG | LEG | LEG | //// |

10-foot 2x6

| ARM | ARM | ARM | ARM | FOOT | FOOT | FOOT | FOOT | // |

6-foot 2x4

| TOP PIECE | TOP PIECE | // |

6-foot 2x4

| TOP PIECE | TOP PIECE | // |

6-foot 2x8

| TOP PIECE | TOP PIECE | // |

# PROJECT ALTERATIONS

PROJECT ALTERATIONS

The trestle bench, page 25, worked so well that I took the remaining leftover pieces of wood from the same deck—slightly bigger and a bit more valuable—and dreamed up something larger. It looks more like a standard bench squared off at the ends. Though constructed without using huge pieces of lumber, this bench provides an impressively wide surface. As well, the same design features that join the pieces side to side to create that width also give the bench incredible strength along its length. I've since built benches of the same design up to 8 feet long, and they show no sign of sagging in the middle. The bench also looks well proportioned in lengths of 5 feet and 6 feet, but the original was 4 feet, once again a length dictated by the available material. Whatever length you prefer, simply cut the top pieces and one 2x6 brace to that length, then cut the 2x6 bottom brace approximately 3 inches (the total thickness of the two end pieces) shorter.

This bench derives its strength from the fact that one of the top boards combines with the two braces underneath to form an I-shaped beam. I-beams provide exceptional rigidity: to attain the maximum strength with minimum weight, steel is shaped into I-beams when wide spans are necessary. In the case of the bench, think of it this way: if the seat wants to sag under the weight of too many people, the vertical brace beneath it has to bend into a curve, and to do that, it has to stretch along its bottom edge. The 2x6 attached below prevents it from doing so, which is why it is important to screw the two braces at close intervals.

The same I-shaped structure that lends strength also braces the bench and prevents it from racking. One traditional bench design

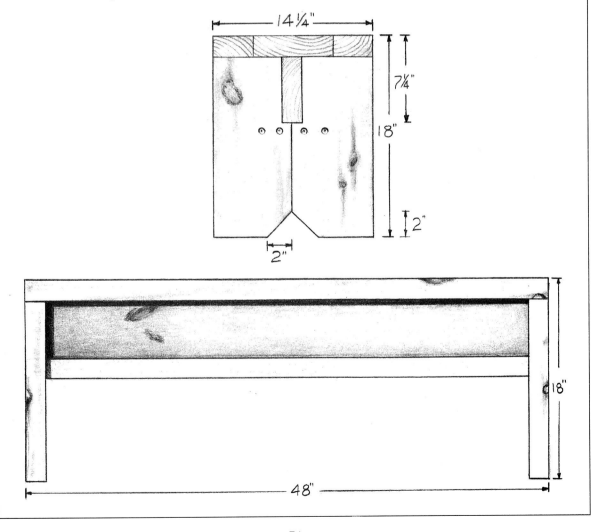

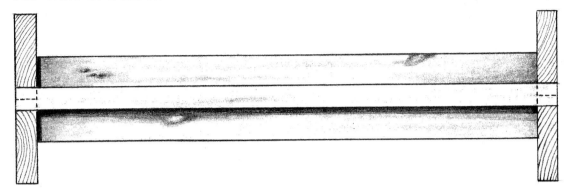

achieves these same qualities by installing diagonal struts from the midpoint on the seat to each leg. The I-beam simply straightens out the diagonals and braces the bench from end to end.

1 To begin, cut all pieces to length, and sand everything before you assemble the bench. Clamp the four end pieces together, and cut identical notches in each of them. (See "Cutting Notches," page 26.) The notches should be exactly half the thickness of the 2x6 brace, which will fit into the slot created when two end pieces are placed side by side.

2 With the notches cut, attach the vertical 2x6 brace to one of the 2x8 leg pieces at each end. Use #8 2½-inch wood screws and waterproof glue. Screw through the 2x6 into the

## SCREW ANGLES

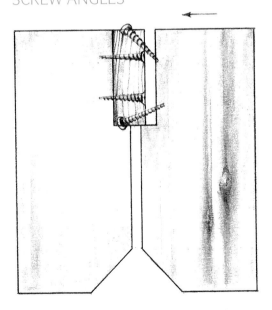

2x8 leg member; the end of the brace should be flush with the outside of the leg.

Now attach the other leg member by angling screws into it through the vertical brace. Start the screws from the edges of the brace (the 2-inch dimension) so that the screws will not be visible on the finished bench. Drill small pilot holes to ease the installation of these awkwardly angled screws.

3 In order to match the width of the legs, the top of the bench should be made from two 2x8s, one of which has been ripped along its length into two equal halves. One 2x8 and two 2x4s will work almost as well, but since a 2x4 is not as wide as half a 2x8, either the legs will have to be planed down a fraction of an inch once the bench is assembled, or you will need to leave a slightly larger gap between the top pieces to make up the difference in size. The important thing about the top, however, is simply that the vertical brace below is covered by the centre top board.

Install the top pieces so that they line up flush with the legs on both the sides and the ends, and screw them in place using #8 2½-inch wood screws, seven at each end of the bench. Predrill holes through the top boards so that the screws do not split the grain, and countersink the holes.

4 With the top firmly attached, turn the bench upside down, and join the bottom brace to the lower edge of the vertical brace with four evenly spaced wood screws.

5 Drive screws from the outside of *all four* leg pieces into the bottom brace.

Like the trestle bench, the I-beam bench can

be thrown together in a big hurry and fastened with 2½-inch galvanized ardox nails if all you want is something rough and ready. The design has enough structural strength and mass that even the most rigorous use won't break it down. And in such cases, pressure-treated wood (PT) will suffice as long as you keep in mind that the chemicals in PT are not appropriate for tabletops or benches that might, for example, get used by kids as an impromptu table.

## GLUES

*There are more adhesives available than you can shake a glue brush at, plus numerous brand names of each variety. There are, in other words, more kinds of glue than you will ever need. Ignore most of them.*

*For outdoor furniture, buy a waterproof glue that provides strength. Do not use white carpenter's glue or any of its yellow- and brown-toned cousins; even after it is set, a good soaking turns such glue back into mush.*

*EPOXY*

*Anyone who can afford it should use a two-part epoxy. It has legendary strength; mixed properly, it retains limited flexibility. It can be purchased in a "5-minute" form that sets while you wait and allows you to carry right on with your projects. And while many glues claim to produce a bond stronger than the surrounding wood, only epoxy consistently delivers such adhesion.*

*Epoxy is the most expensive of the outdoor glues, but it also provides good value. It dries clear. After you apply clamps, allow any squeeze-out to set, and then break or sand it off. Mix epoxy in plastic dairy-product containers; they are just about the only thing in your workshop that epoxy will not stick to.*

*RESORCINOL*

*Used in marine and aircraft construction, this is another well-known waterproof glue that resists extreme conditions. It sets to an appealing dark maroon colour (a friend once used it to pour a dark inlay in the top of a box he had made and carved), but that of course means that the finest gaps in your joints will be highlighted by a conspicuous glue line. Like epoxy, resorcinol can be quite expensive, and also like epoxy, it requires the user to mix together two components, in this case a powder and a viscous fluid. But it sets hard and fills gaps well. After clamping, clean up carefully, or you will smear a finish-resistant mess around the joint.*

*POWDERED UREA*

*Sometimes sold under the self-explanatory names "Waterproof Glue" or "Plastic Resin Glue," powdered-urea resin glues are another suitable adhesive for the* projects contained in this book. Like resorcinol, it sets to a more brittle state than epoxy. It is not, therefore, the first choice for a dining chair that may have to endure considerable movement, but it works well in every other application here. When I asked for opinions at the lumberyard, they suggested plastic resin, pointing out that in addition to its strength and weatherproof durability, it costs only a quarter as much as resorcinol. Water-mixed plastic resin glue wipes up easily with a wet rag and produces a tan-coloured glue line.*

*Whichever you choose, read the instructions. Temperature and humidity affect almost all glues, and the mixing proportions for epoxy and resorcinol are crucial. By varying the amounts of epoxy resin and hardener, you can produce glues with markedly different traits. In the extreme, one of those traits is that it sets instantly, producing a casting of your mixing cup with the stir stick jutting out like a lollipop handle and generating enough heat to make you drop the whole thing.*

*A couple of additional notes: Common wisdom once held that the two surfaces to be glued should be roughened slightly. Tests have now determined that this is not necessary for most glues, although some epoxy technical manuals still recommend using 80-grit sandpaper to create an abraded surface that the glue keys into.*

*In a few places, the plans in this book call for end grain to butt against side grain or long grain where two pieces meet to form a corner. Even with all the progress that has been made in adhesives, this remains a notoriously poor glue joint. It should be supplemented with fasteners (nails or screws), and wherever possible, it should also be braced with a block arranged so that the corner being glued is also held by the glue joints between the **sides** of the block and the **sides** of the two pieces.*

*When you must glue end grain, "double-bond" the joint by applying two coats, one to fill voids in the end grain and the second to make the actual joint.*

# CUTTING DIAGRAM AND MATERIALS LIST

## MATERIALS LIST

one 8-foot 2x8
one 6-foot 2x8
one 8-foot 2x6

2½" #8 wood screws
  or 2½" galvanized ardox nails
waterproof glue

## PARTS LIST

| | |
|---|---|
| 2 top pieces | 2x4x48" |
| 1 top piece | 2x8x48" |
| 4 leg pieces | 2x8x16" |
| 1 vertical brace | 2x6x48" |
| 1 horizontal brace | 2x6x44"-44½"* |

*depending on thickness of material

## CUTTING DIAGRAM

8-foot 2x8

| TOP PIECE | TOP PIECE |
|---|---|
| | TOP PIECE |

6-foot 2x8

| LEG | LEG | LEG | LEG | |
|---|---|---|---|---|

8-foot 2x6

| VERTICAL BRACE | HORIZONTAL BRACE | |
|---|---|---|

# PROJECT ALTERATIONS

The skirt bench derives its strength from two boards set on edge and notched into the legs, bracing the top along its length. This bench, too, can be easily modified and built in a variety of lengths, and again, the dimensions of the one I put together followed from the length of the board I had available—in this case, a 2x12 chunk of spruce 4 feet long. Make the top approximately 2½ inches longer than the braces, and cut the legs to 16 inches or to a length 1½ inches shorter than any other benches you already have so that the top of your new bench will come out to a matching height.

1 Begin by cutting everything to length, and then decide how you want the vertical braces to look. Typically, they end with a curve resembling the profile of a giant cove moulding, but they can also be sawed off straight or at an angle. (See illustrations on next page.) I traced the curve for mine using the edge of a large bucket of drywall compound sitting in the corner of the shop. The bucket is a standard size and has a diameter of 9 inches, but you can make your own decision about the look you find most pleasing and shape the braces accordingly.

2 Next, cut the notches in the sides of the legs. (See "Cutting Notches," page 26.) The vertical braces are 1x6, and the precise dimension of those braces will determine the dimensions of the notches. If you chose to score the bottom of the piece that will form the top of the bench to minimize warping, do so now. (See "Milling Grooves," page 60.)

3 Assemble all the parts, spreading glue in the notches before installing the skirts. Fasten everything with #8 2½-inch wood screws or 2½-inch galvanized ardox nails.

The skirt bench can be made from smaller stock than a 2x12, but it will become tippy as the top and legs become narrower. To fix this problem, cut the legs another 1½ inches shorter and attach feet cut from a piece of 2x4 to the bottom of each leg. The feet can be cut to any length you desire but should

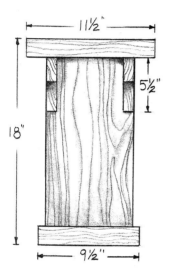

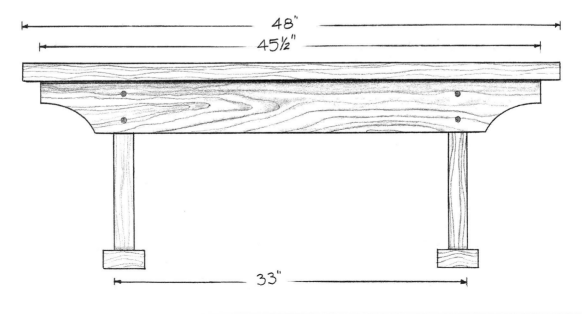

## THE SCRAP PILE

*Any confirmed shop fool already knows about the scrap pile: that's where every off-cut longer than 8 inches languishes until the day you need just such a piece to finish your current project. The scrap pile, however, can also supply you with an entire materials list. I built each of the original benches described using wood left over from grander designs. Look in your scrap pile before you begin any of these projects, and if necessary, modify plans to accommodate the materials you already have.*

*As well, keep your eyes open for construction sites with a pile of scraps out front. For many contractors, that mound of 2x4, 2x6, 2x8 and 2x10 pieces is nothing more than a nuisance. They'll thank you for taking it away before they have to pay to get it dumped. In*

*some areas, the lumber will be spruce—hardly the longest-lasting material, but if all you need it for are some rough benches or a table base, the savings will offset the possible inconvenience of having to replace them some years down the road. Never, of course, take anything without asking.*

*And if you see someone building a cedar or redwood deck, stop your car, run directly over and ask for scraps. You can usually build a whole gallery's worth of benches from the off-cuts of a good-sized deck. Nothing could be better: you save money, you prevent wood and trees from going to waste, you save someone a few pounds' worth of tipping fees at the nearest transfer station, and you reduce the burden on your local landfill by at least a few boards.*

not be longer than the top is wide, or else you will stub your toe on them far too often. Attach the feet with more glue and countersunk #8 3-inch wood screws.

Such an arrangement has the added advantage that the side grain of the 2x4 feet will be far less absorbent than the end grain of the legs. A bench used outside often rots from the bottom up because the legs have wicked moisture from the earth. Every now and then, you will see an old bench that sits extraordinarily close to the ground. Perhaps it is another case of people being smaller a couple of generations

ago, but chances are that some enterprising handyperson has simply trimmed off the damaged wood at the ends of the legs. You can bring these benches back up to a more comfortable height by tacking on some 2x4 feet.

Here's a good piece of advice: Whatever length you make your benches, first measure the long side of every table—inside your house and out—that might someday need extra seating. If you have more friends and family than you have chairs and piano stools, then you should make sure your benches don't end up 3 inches too long to fit at the dining tables.

## VERTICAL BRACE OR SKIRT SHAPES

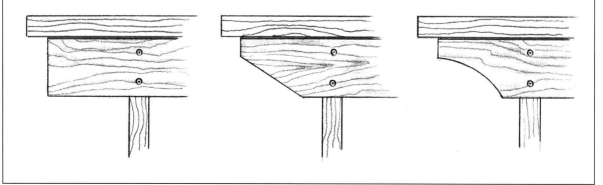

## MATERIALS LIST

one 4-foot 2x12
one 4-foot 2x8
one 4-foot 1x10
two scraps 2x4x9½"

2½" #8 wood screws
3" #8 wood screws
  or 2½" galvanized ardox nails
waterproof glue

## PARTS LIST

| | |
|---|---|
| 1 top piece | 2x12x48" |
| 2 legs | 2x8x16" |
| 2 skirts | 1x4½x45½" |
| *optional:* | |
| 2 feet | 2x4x9½" |

## CUTTING DIAGRAM

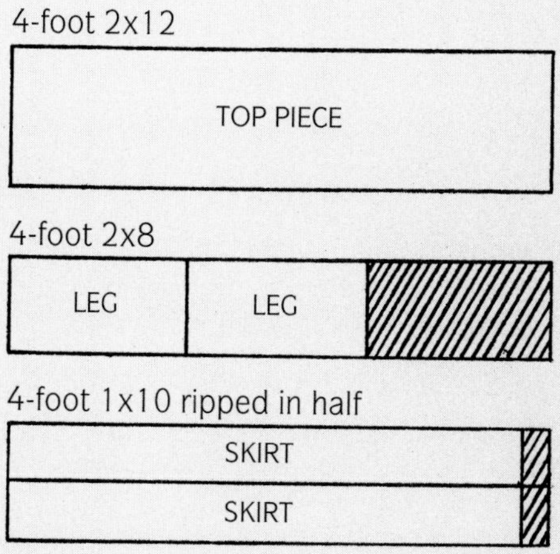

4-foot 2x12

```
┌──────────────────────────────┐
│                              │
│          TOP PIECE           │
│                              │
└──────────────────────────────┘
```

4-foot 2x8

```
┌──────────┬──────────┬─────────┐
│   LEG    │   LEG    │/////////│
└──────────┴──────────┴─────────┘
```

4-foot 1x10 ripped in half

```
┌───────────────────────┬──┐
│         SKIRT         │//│
├───────────────────────┼──┤
│         SKIRT         │//│
└───────────────────────┴──┘
```

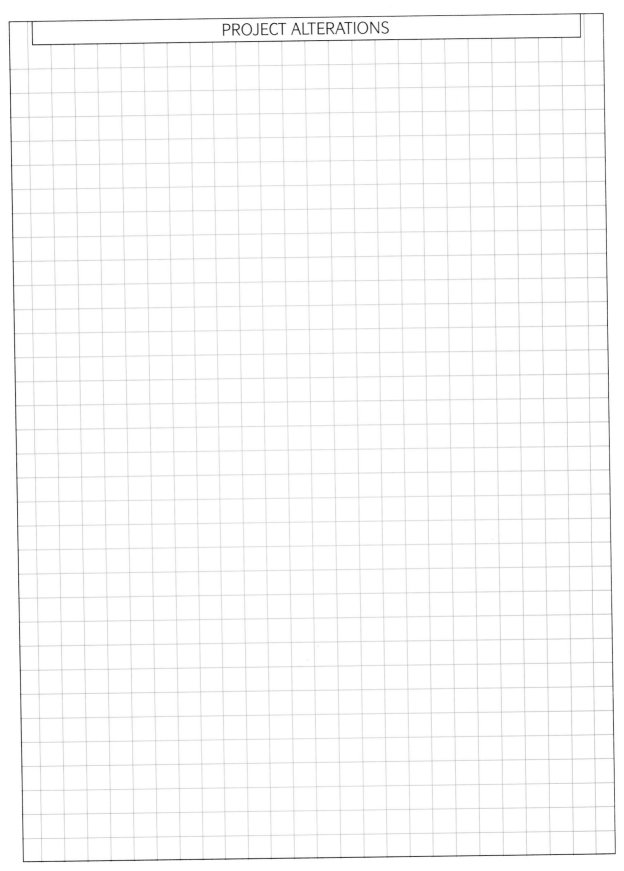

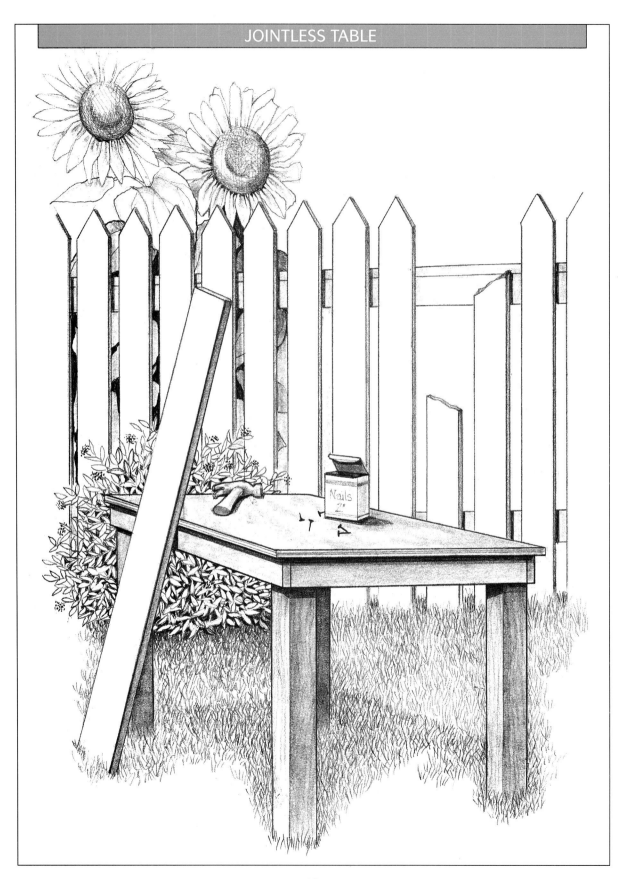

The plans set out here for a jointless table serve two purposes. First, you might want to build one, especially if you need a backyard work area and feel you can get by with something a bit rough. Second, a jointless table highlights the problems that good table design must overcome—even if you decide you want to move on to some of the other table plans contained in this book, pause here first to see what you are gaining by your extra work. As well, with a few adjustments, you can transform this table into a potting bench, complete with shelves above and below for dirt and tools and containers.

1 Begin with the legs. If you want to dress things up a little, search in your local lumberyards for pressure-treated, preturned newel posts, which are fancier than a plain 4x4. Use them upside down; that is, with the rounded top serving as the foot of the leg. Given the techniques you'll be using, this will be a little like making a sow's ear out of a silk purse, but the preturned, dried and pressure-treated posts will be less likely to twist than lengths of standard lumber, and that counts very much in their favour. Cut the legs to a length of 29 inches. If you use newel posts, remember to trim from the end that has been squared off, leaving the decorative rounded end intact.

2 Cut the aprons to the dimensions you prefer. A standard finished tabletop of 3 feet by 5 feet works well and is probably as large as you should go. With an overhang of 2 inches all the way around, that means you want side aprons measuring 56 inches and end aprons measuring 30 inches.

3 Apply waterproof glue, then nail or screw the *end* pieces onto the legs so that they rest flush with the outside edges of the legs.

4 Apply more waterproof glue, and nail or screw the *sides* so that they extend to rest flush with the outside edges of the end aprons. In both cases, do your gluing and nailing or screwing with all possible care. These connections are the weak points in the jointless design. Whatever pressure is on the table to twist or rack in any direction will work on these corners, and all that holds things together are the connectors you install. As well, weight placed on the top of the table bears straight down on the connection between the aprons and legs, and in large measure, that weight will be resting on the screws or nails.

5 With the table upside down, measure the diagonals (from the inside of one leg to the inside of its opposite diagonal). If the structure is perfectly rectangular, the diagonals will be equal; if it has slipped over into a parallelogram, they will not. Adjust the table until the diagonals are equal, then tack small temporary braces across the corners to keep everything square as you turn the table upright.

6 Now nail on a top of either 1-inch or ⁵⁄₄-inch lumber or, if this is to be a rough work surface, plywood. If you choose a lighter material, add a stringer under the tabletop first. Use the same material as the aprons, and cut it to the same length as the end aprons. Locate

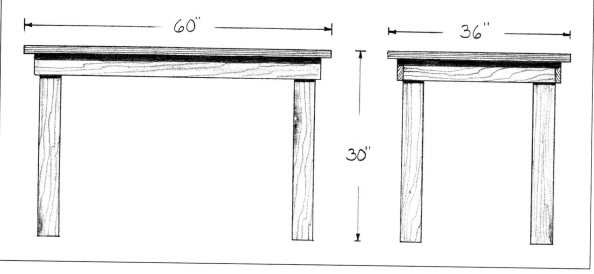

the stringer under the middle of the top, and attach it to the side aprons with 2-inch nails or #8 2-inch screws before nailing or screwing the top boards to it and to the end and side aprons.

If your lumber is good and dry, paint everything before assembly, except the places to which you want to apply glue. Otherwise, wait until the sun dries the finished piece entirely.

## CORNER BRACKETS

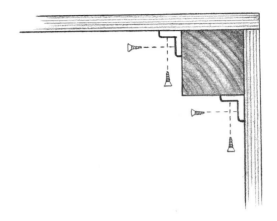

7   Finally, turn the table upside down again, and angle two screws (not nails) up through the inside surfaces of each leg and into the top pieces of the table.

It should not take much more than an hour to put together a jointless table. If it turns out better than you expected and you decide to build in some extra stiffness to the table and perhaps extend its life expectancy, you can add two 1½-by-1½-inch inside corner brackets to each leg to brace the connections between the aprons and the legs.

## POTTING BENCH

To convert your jointless table to a down-and-dirty potting bench, simply use longer material for the rear legs and allow the 4x4s to project 3 feet above the level of the tabletop. Surface the table with a single piece of ¾-inch exterior-grade plywood cut to fit around the extended rear legs, and either trim the edges of the plywood with wood and paint the top surface, or cover the top with seamless flooring material or with real ceramic tiles properly cemented and grouted into place.

Follow the instructions contained in "Cutting Notches" on page 26 to cut 1½-by-1½-inch notches in the 4x4s above where they project through the work surface. You can cut either a single set of notches approximately 30 inches above the work surface or two sets at approximately 12 inches and 24 inches. Each set of notches will accept either a 2x6 or a 2x8 to serve as shelf space. Apply glue to all three surfaces of each notch, and countersink some 3½-inch screws through from the outside of the 4x4 uprights to snug everything up tight.

For additional storage down below, connect each back leg to its corresponding front leg with 2x4s cut to the same length as the end aprons above, and either place another sheet of plywood across these or fasten pieces of 1-inch or 2-inch material in place to create the shelf (use the heavier planks if you plan to store large clay pots and/or bags of potting soil). Fasten with nails or screws.

If you have a deck or a wooden fence around your yard, you can treat the ends of the extended 4x4s in the same manner as the posts in the fence or deck; that is, you can top them with turned caps or by cutting them at an angle all the way around. Fancy post tops are available at most lumberyards.

## POTTING BENCH

# CUTTING DIAGRAM AND MATERIALS LIST

## MATERIALS LIST

two 6-foot 4x4s
one 10-foot ⁵⁄₄x4
one 8-foot ⁵⁄₄x4
two 10-foot 1x6s
one 6-foot 1x6
one 6-foot 1x8

3" #8 wood screws
1½"x1½" corner brackets
2" #8 wood screws
   or 2" galvanized ardox nails
3½" #8 wood screws
   or 3½" galvanized ardox nails
waterproof glue

## PARTS LIST

| | |
|---|---:|
| 4 legs | 4x4x29" |
| 2 side aprons | ⁵⁄₄x4x56" |
| 2 end aprons | ⁵⁄₄x4x30" |
| 1 stringer | ⁵⁄₄x4x30" |
| 5 top pieces | 1x6x60" |
| 1 top piece | 1x8x60" |
| *optional:* | |
| 1 top piece | 36"x60" plywood |

## CUTTING DIAGRAM

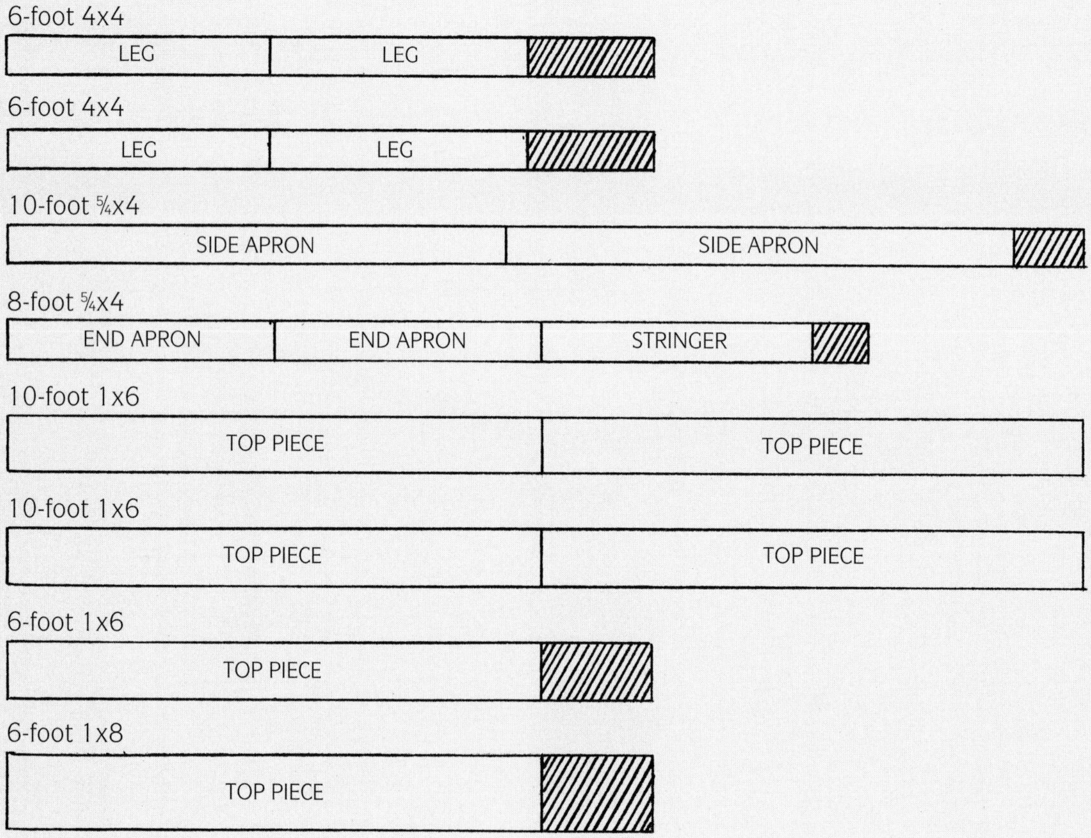

6-foot 4x4

| LEG | LEG | |
|---|---|---|

6-foot 4x4

| LEG | LEG | |
|---|---|---|

10-foot ⁵⁄₄x4

| SIDE APRON | SIDE APRON | |
|---|---|---|

8-foot ⁵⁄₄x4

| END APRON | END APRON | STRINGER | |
|---|---|---|---|

10-foot 1x6

| TOP PIECE | TOP PIECE |
|---|---|

10-foot 1x6

| TOP PIECE | TOP PIECE |
|---|---|

6-foot 1x6

| TOP PIECE | |
|---|---|

6-foot 1x8

| TOP PIECE | |
|---|---|

# PROJECT ALTERATIONS

The chairs, benches and tables that make up most of the projects in this book do the usual things in the usual ways and do not require much discussion, but planter boxes come with a little bit of gardening theory.

First of all, unless you expect to raise a tree in your planter box, it probably needs far less room for earth than many of the freestanding boxes you have seen. Most flowers and vegetables—with the exception of carrots and others of that ilk—do not put down roots to a great depth. Basil or pansies or lavender require only a few inches of dirt, and since the less you put in a planter, the easier it will be to move and the longer it will last, it is worth giving some thought to minimizing the actual earth compartment in the box you build. That's the first thing. The second is this: too little earth will allow the container to dry out quickly under the summer sun, and your plants will suffer something called drought stress. Do not make your container less than 8 inches deep.

What follows are plans for a planter that will be large enough to fill a spot on the corner of your deck but still light enough to move around, with enough capacity to grow just about anything. Like other plans in this book, however, these can be modified and, in this case, made up to half again as large in all dimensions while still remaining structurally sound. If you need a container that holds more earth, the bottom can be installed at whatever depth you require.

The dimensions given here derive from the fact that the pieces of 1x6 tongue-and-groove V-joint cedar that I purchased for the sides were exactly 5 inches wide plus the tongue. That meant the space between the legs was best set at a multiple of 5 inches, and everything else followed from that. The ends are 10 inches (plus legs) wide, and the sides are 25 inches (plus legs) long. I made the legs 17¼ inches so that, with the ¾-inch top, the planter came out the same height as the benches described on pages 25-38.

I selected a finish trim called bed moulding, but almost any cedar trim will do. Choose something that suits you.

1 Begin by building the legs. These, like the legs for the harvest table on page 56, are assembled from two pieces butted together to give the appearance of being a solid chunk of wood while providing two inside surfaces to which the cross members/stringers can be attached. If you want the legs to be exactly the same width on the sides as the front, begin with a 2x6, and rip it so that you end up with two pieces, one of which is narrower than the other by exactly the thickness of the original piece. (See illustration on next page.) If your 2x6 measures 1½ inches by 5½ inches, for example, rip it into a 2-inch piece and a 3½-inch piece (split the difference of the ⅛-inch sawcut). If you are not so fussy, simply use 2x2s and 2x4s in the same manner. Cut the legs to a finished length of 17¼ inches.

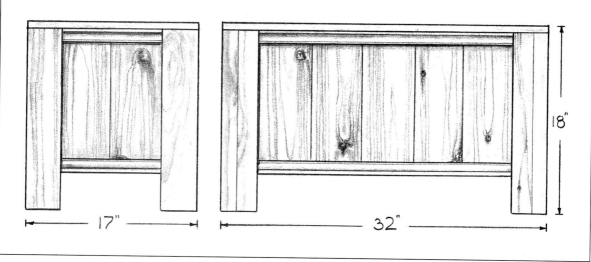

17"          32"          18"

49

Mix up some waterproof glue, and use lots as you butt the leg pieces together; attach them with 2½-inch galvanized ardox nails or three #8 2½-inch wood screws.

There is nothing delicate about the legs at this point, so you do not need to let the glue dry before carrying on. It doesn't matter whether you lay out the legs with the joint showing to the side or to the ends, but be consistent.

2 Measure down from the top of each leg, and mark the inside at 13 inches. (This is one of the dimensions of the plan that is easily modified. If you want a shallower box, measure down and mark off 10 inches; adjust the length of the side pieces accordingly.)

3 Lay the legs out on a bench in pairs so that you have exactly the desired gap between them for the tongue-and-groove side pieces (25 inches). Now take precise measurements of the distance between the inside corners of the legs, and cut the four stringers you will need from the 1x3 material. Predrill pilot holes at the ends of the stringers, and attach the stringers to the legs with more glue and #8 1¾-inch wood screws. The top stringer should rest flush with the top of the legs, and the bottom edge of the bottom stringer should line up with the line you marked. Be sure the stringers are perpendicular to the legs. Double-check for square by measuring the diagonals when you finish, and make any necessary adjustments.

4 Turn the two side assemblies up on their ends now so that, once again, you leave the exact required gap between them where the end pieces will be installed (10 inches, or the size dictated by your materials). Again, measure the exact distance between the inside corners of the legs, and cut stringers to fit. Install them just as you did the sides, using glue and #8 1¾-inch wood screws. Check for square by measuring the diagonals.

5 At this stage, you have the frame of a box, and if anything is out of kilter, now is the time to wrestle it into shape. Before the glue dries, there will still be some flexibility in the fasteners. Once you are satisfied that all is as it should be, cut the tongue-and-groove boards to the same length as the measurement from the top of the top stringer to the bottom of the bottom stringer. You measured this dimension onto the legs yourself, so it should still be exactly 13 inches, but if it is not, adjust the lengths of tongue-and-groove accordingly.

6 Take a moment to examine the tongue-and-groove V-joint before you install it. There is often a pronounced grain in contrasting shades, and you can sometimes enhance the visual effect by alternating the different colours.

Dry-fit the boards in place, beginning with a groove side placed against one leg. You will notice that you have to remove the tongue from

TOP VIEW SHOWING TONGUE-AND-GROOVE

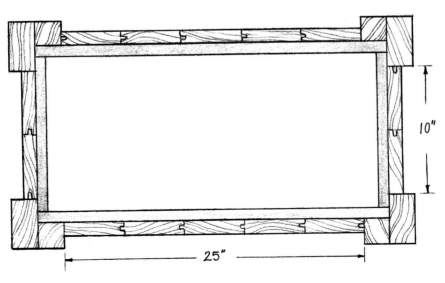

10"

25"

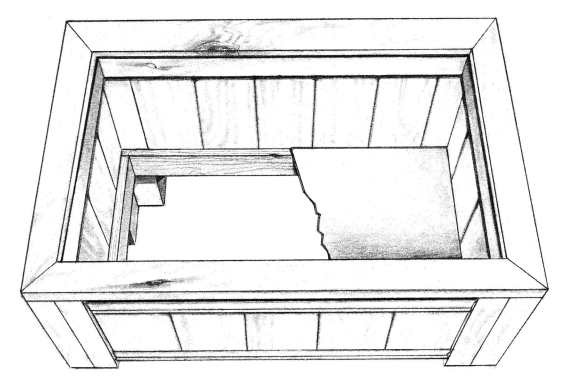

the last piece where it fits against the second leg. Install the V-joint tongue-and-groove using lots of glue and 1¼-inch finishing nails (if you prefer wood screws, use #6 size and predrill the holes). Drive three evenly spaced nails through each end of the boards, not through the tongue as you normally would with tongue-and-groove; the trim pieces will cover the nailheads. You may need a brace behind the stringer as you bang in the nails.

7 Use the remaining 1x3 to install a top that covers the edge of the top stringer, the end grain of the V-joint tongue-and-groove and the legs. It should be flush with the inside of the box. Mitre the corners, and spread lots more glue before you nail the top pieces down with 1¾-inch finishing nails. Be sure to glue the mitre joints while you are at it. Set all the nails carefully, since cedar lumber is notorious for varying in thickness, and you may have to plane the top pieces so that they meet smoothly at the corners. You don't want to trim any nailheads with your block plane. If anything, plane a very slight bevel onto the top so that it sheds water.

8 Install the trim so that it fits up under the lip of the top piece and along the bottom edge of the tongue-and-groove. Do not use your measuring tape; simply hold the trim up to the space it will fill, and mark it directly for each cut. Use more glue and more 1¾-inch finishing nails.

9 Finally, take measurements of the inside of the box so that you can cut the bottom from a chunk of ½- or ¾-inch plywood. Since you want the bottom piece to rest on the top of the bottom side stringers, it should be cut to the full inside *width* of the box. It will have to be slightly shorter than the inside length of the box so that you can fit it in there. Drill holes through the bottom piece so that the box can drain. If you have no plywood handy and do not want to buy a half sheet just for the bottom, pieces of 2-inch lumber will do; gaps between the pieces will provide drainage.

10 Set the finishing nails, and fill the holes; a wax-finish repair pencil, available at lumberyards, will do the job, or you can use wood filler—but first see "Wood Fillers and Countersunk Holes," page 61.

When it comes time to fill your planter, put a layer of foam packing peanuts in the bottom for drainage. They are much lighter than crushed stone, and this is the only good use they have now that some mail-order house has delivered them to your home stuffed around the barbecue you ordered.

## A SHALLOWER BOX

If you want to create a planter with a substantial appearance but a minimum of earth inside, you can build your box to the dimensions described above and then install two additional side stringers to support the bottom at a shallower depth. The extra stringers present none of the usual worry about adding weight to the structure, since they make it possible to leave out a much heavier volume of moist earth.

Also, keep in mind that instead of filling the completed box with drainage material and earth, you can provide all the soil some plants need by setting a couple of plastic pots inside the finished planter. If you find the right size, they will not show at all; everything will be that much easier to move, and the planter will last longer for being kept out of contact with the potting soil.

# CUTTING DIAGRAM AND MATERIALS LIST

## MATERIALS LIST

one 6-foot 2x6
one 8-foot 1x6
one 6-foot 1x6
two 8-foot pieces 1x6 V-joint
   tongue-and-groove
two 8-foot pieces bed moulding

2½" #8 wood screws
1¾" #8 wood screws
1¼" finishing nails
1¾" finishing nails
waterproof glue

## PARTS LIST

| | |
|---|---|
| 4 leg pieces | 2x4x17¼" |
| 4 leg pieces | 2x2x17¼" |
| 2 top trim pieces | 1x3x32½" |
| 2 top trim pieces | 1x3x17½" |
| 4 inside stringers | 1x3x27½" |
| 4 inside stringers | 1x3x13½" |
| 14 side pieces | 1x6x13" |
| 4 side trim pieces bed moulding | 10" |
| 4 side trim pieces bed moulding | 25" |

## CUTTING DIAGRAM

**6-foot 2x6**

| LEG PIECE | LEG PIECE | LEG PIECE | LEG PIECE | |
| LEG PIECE | LEG PIECE | LEG PIECE | LEG PIECE | |

**8-foot 1x6 ripped in half**

| TOP TRIM | TOP TRIM | INSIDE STRINGER | |
| INSIDE STRINGER | INSIDE STRINGER | INSIDE STRINGER | | INSIDE STRINGER |

**6-foot 1x6 ripped in half**

| TOP TRIM | TOP TRIM | INSIDE STRINGERS | |
INSIDE STRINGER

**8-foot 1x6 V-joint tongue-and-groove**

| SIDE PIECE | SIDE PIECE | SIDE PIECE | SIDE PIECE | SIDE PIECE | SIDE PIECE | SIDE PIECE | |

**8-foot 1x6 V-joint tongue-and-groove**

| SIDE PIECE | SIDE PIECE | SIDE PIECE | SIDE PIECE | SIDE PIECE | SIDE PIECE | SIDE PIECE | |

**8-foot bed moulding**

| TRIM | TRIM | TRIM | TRIM | TRIM | |

**8-foot bed moulding**

| TRIM | TRIM | TRIM | |

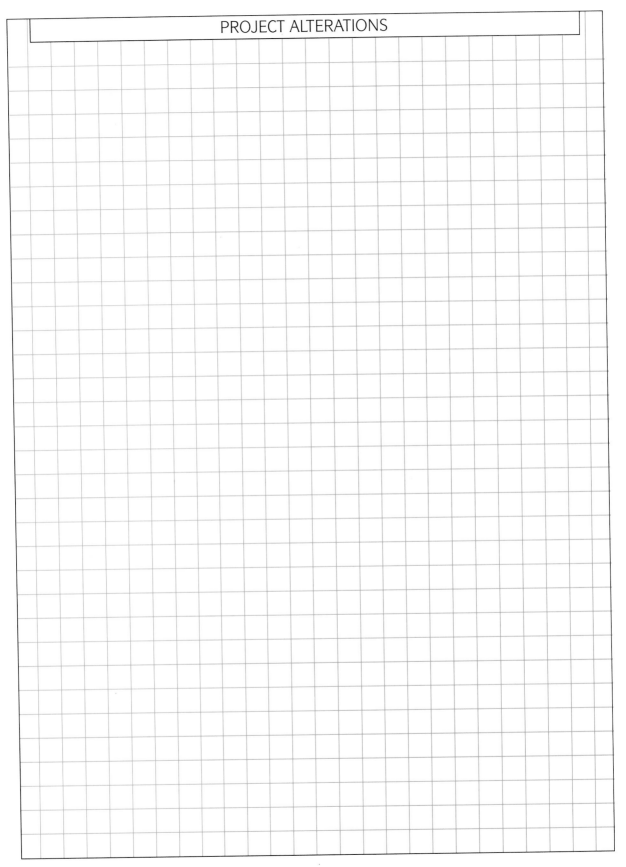

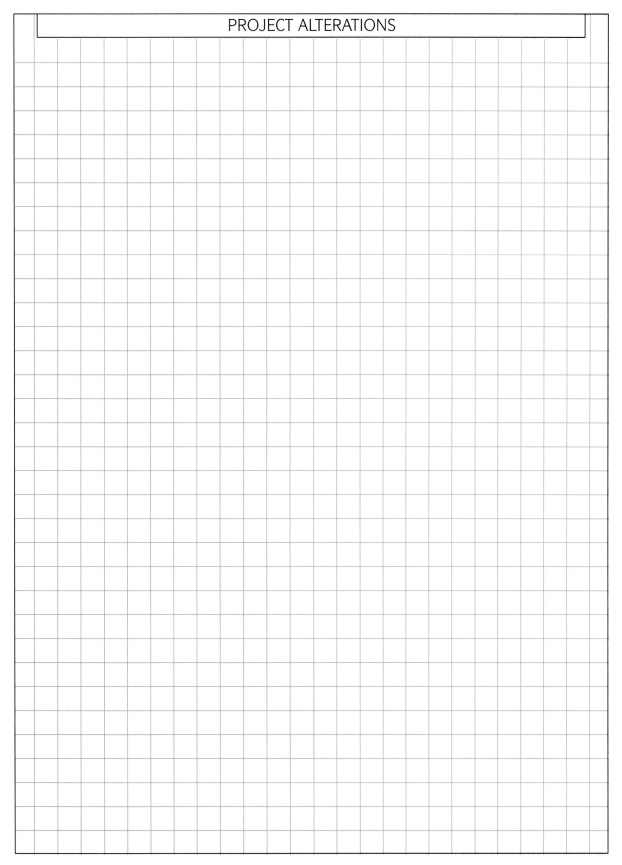

When the table described below was all done, I showed it to a friend of mine. Steve is a woodworker. He is also an architectural technologist, which is why the first thing he did after running his hand once over the tabletop was to squat down and look at the underside where everything hangs together. After thinking for a moment, he pointed to the little blocks that hold up the aprons (the sides of the table) and cleared his throat like someone who has bad news.

"These could have been bigger," he said. "In fact, they could have gone all the way to the bottom of the leg."

I nodded. They are only a couple of inches long and just 2 inches square, and I originally considered making them full length, because the blocks are held up only by the screws and glue attaching them to the legs. Certainly the tabletop would be better supported if the load were transferred all the way to the ground. Still, I was about to defend my decision when Steve came to the same conclusion I had.

"But this isn't a house, after all," he said, standing up.

This isn't really a harvest table after all either, though it looks like an expensive reproduction and might actually be too good to be left outside. It would be right at home in a large kitchen, and it has room around it for half a dozen regular dining room chairs. It is, however, easy to build, and with careful gluing and a sturdy finish, it should withstand outdoor use as well as anything else made out of wood does.

Like most of the projects in this book, the harvest table requires no joinery. While there are numerous ways that carefully cut joints can be useful in constructing a table, many have to do with aesthetics and are not necessary for its function. A table, after all, simply bears a weight that pushes directly down onto the legs. There is a broad surface over which to distribute that weight, and each of the four legs performs exactly one-quarter of the total task. And unlike the load in a chair, the weight on a table rarely fidgets and never tips itself up on the back legs.

Traditionally, however, harvest tables use a mortise-and-tenon joint to connect the aprons to each leg, and it is worth understanding what you give up by substituting another construction. Unlike the design below, the traditional harvest table has solid legs, and the ends of the aprons run into those legs; the mortise-and-tenon arrangement makes it possible to connect the ends of the aprons to the uprights. This accomplishes three things: One, the weight carried by the aprons hangs from the tenons where they fit inside the mortises; two, the sides of the tenon, called "cheeks," provide ample long-grain gluing surfaces; and three, the shoulders of the tenons prevent movement that would damage the glue joint. To better understand the importance of the shoulders of a mortise-and-tenon (tab and slot) joint, examine the trestle table on page 78. The shoulders cut onto the long stringer provide stability for that structure in just the same way.

Each of those functions has to be replaced in order for the table to hold its weight. Because the legs of the table below are not solid but

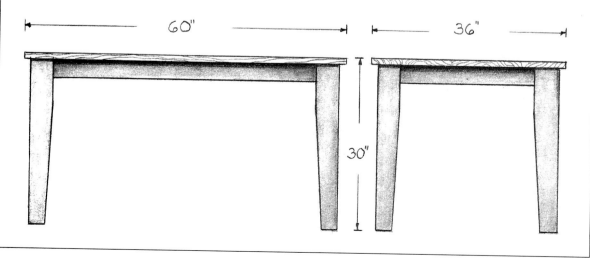

instead consist of two pieces forming a right angle, there is ample exposed side grain to which the aprons can be glued. To prevent movement, the apron assembly must fit as tightly into the inside corners of the legs as the shoulders of a tenon fit against the surface around a mortise. And to carry the weight from above, the blocks installed beneath the aprons on the inside angle of the legs must also fit precisely. Keep the ideal of a perfect mortise-and-tenon in mind as you work through the instructions below.

1 The Aprons: Lay out the four pieces for the apron assembly on a flat work surface, and drill countersunk pilot holes at the ends of the longer side aprons. Spread glue (either resorcinol or epoxy, which I used because my friend Bob had some mixed up for the canoe stems he was building) on the end grain of the shorter end aprons, and join them together using #8 1¾-inch wood screws. Once all four corners are screwed together, measure the diagonals to be sure you have created a proper rectangle and not some more exotic geometric quadrangle. If you need to force the pieces into square, tack light braces across one or two of the corners, or clamp the assembly to the work surface while it sets with everything in its proper place.

2 Once the glue sets, cut four small blocks (1x1 or 2x2) that match the width of the aprons, and using more glue and countersunk screws, set one of these inside each of the four corners to provide bracing and a gluing surface. These are the real strength of the corners. If you prefer, you can cut longer braces with 45-degree angles on the ends and install these at each corner. Let the glue set again.

3 Install the stringer at the halfway point using more glue and a pair of #8 2½-inch wood screws at each end driven through the aprons into the end grain of the stringer. Keeping in mind that glue and screws into end grain do not provide an ideal joint, you can also brace the connection with four more small blocks glued into place at the junction of the stringer and the aprons.

4 The Legs: These legs are like the buildings on a movie set—they look solid, but they aren't. Instead of consisting of a single chunk of 6x6 pine for each leg and a series of mortise-and-tenon joints to connect them to the aprons, these legs are each assembled from two pieces of ⅝-inch stock. This method costs less, it uses wood more responsibly, it reduces the likelihood of cracking or checking that occurs with the larger-dimension lumber, and it simplifies the process of attaching everything together in the end. In practice, it is not as complicated as a written description makes it sound. The only tricky part is that the two pieces which make up each leg are a different width because one of them butts up to the other. (See illustration below.)

If you have access to a table saw, you can use it to cut the two different widths of wood you need to assemble the legs for the harvest table. You have to set everything up only once in order to do so. Adjust the rip fence to the width of the wider of the two sides of the legs, and leave it at that setting. Make the first cut, then turn that wider member up sideways

## CUTTING LEG PIECES

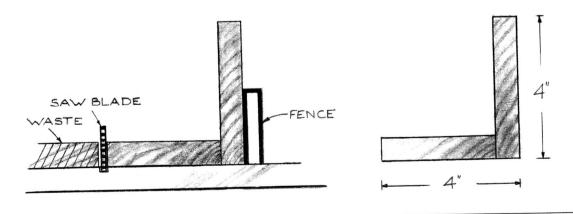

SAW BLADE
WASTE
FENCE
4"
4"

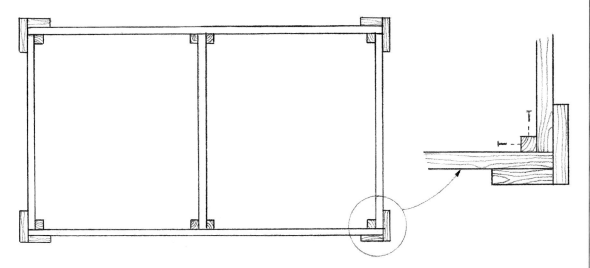

against the fence, and it will provide the exact adjustment you need to cut the narrower portions of the legs.

To give the legs a lighter and more elegant appearance, taper the two pieces before assembling the legs. You can cut whatever taper you prefer, but 1½ inches over 22½ inches works well. Then glue the leg pieces together with epoxy or resorcinol, and clamp them up before you put them aside to set. You can use two or three screws on each leg as well.

5 Once you complete the legs and the apron assembly, find an assistant and assemble the table frame. Begin with everything upside down on a large work surface or flat section of floor. Stand a leg up at each corner

### LEG TAPER

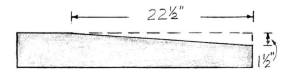

of the apron assembly, and making sure that each leg is in its proper corner (see illustration), mark the inside of the legs so that you know *precisely* where the apron fits.

The blocks that fit inside the legs and support the apron assembly do the lion's share of holding up the tabletop and should be attached

carefully. These are the weak link in the whole design, because most of the weight of the top boards rests on the apron and the aprons sit on the corner blocks, but the blocks themselves merely hang from the legs by four screws each. And glue. The gluing job you do is therefore all-important. And while you have your glue ready and your work standards high, add

### LEG DETAIL

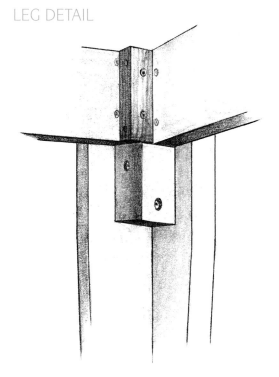

*The proper thing to do with tabletops that you intend to use outdoors is to leave spaces between each of the boards. That way, the expansion and contraction of the materials caused by changes in temperature and moisture conditions will not tear everything apart, and water will have no tight spaces to infiltrate and cause rot. But even when you want the top boards touching along their sides, there is an important technique you can use to counter moisture problems.*

*First, to minimize warping, twisting and cupping, cut two grooves in the underside of each top board. Simply run your circular saw (guided by its fence attachment) along the length of the boards; if you have a table saw with a dado blade, you can produce more effective channels of, say, half an inch in width and half an inch in depth. And if you have a table saw but no dado blade, you can achieve the same effect by setting up a guide so that each board passes across the blade at an angle. The spinning blade will hollow out a rounded furrow; the greater the angle across the blade, the wider the groove. Whatever method you choose, stop the cuts 8 inches in, as you do not want to be able to see these cuts at the edge of the table. By scoring the underside of the boards, you relieve the internal stresses of the wood and allow movement of the fibres without movement of the whole board.*

glue to all points at which the sides of the aprons meet the insides of the legs. Use screws and clamps to make sure that all glued surfaces are drawn into tight contact.

**6** If your shop is not humid and the wood that you plan to use for the top has had time to dry out and shrink, set the boards next to each other, but do not squeeze them tightly together. In other words, allow a bit of room for expansion. If, on the other hand, your shop is damp or if the lumber itself has not dried out, set the boards together as tightly as possible before you fasten them so that any shrinkage will open only minimal cracks between them. In either case, since you are not edge-gluing these boards, it is a good idea to seal the bottoms and sides with at least a sealer/primer before fixing them in place.

Fasten the top boards to the table frame by drilling countersunk holes through from the top and attaching them with #8 2¾-inch wood screws that you drive down into two end aprons and the stringer at the middle of the table. If at this point you are so pleased with the overall effect of your table that you want to lavish extra care on the top, you can cover the holes with real wooden plugs, available from a lumber-supply store, or you can simply fill the holes with wood filler and sand everything flat and smooth.

If you have access to a router, it is a good idea to round the edges of the top. When you are building projects with softwoods such as pine, a curved edge will far better withstand the rough-and-tumble of backyard use. (See "Roundover Bits," page 97.)

# WOOD FILLERS AND COUNTERSUNK HOLES

Some people do not like the heads of screws to show on a finished piece of furniture; the aesthetic effect does not suit their tastes. As well, screwheads can catch on clothing, and unless they are made of brass, they will suffer from the weather. Finally, screwheads can get surprisingly hot under the summer sun—surprising, that is, for the person who sits on one while wearing shorts.

While the obvious thing to do is to countersink the screws, countersinking on outdoor furniture can create problems. Those small holes not only lower the heads of the fasteners, they also create little rainwater reservoirs all over your finished piece. Water collecting there guarantees corrosion of the screws and encourages the various forms of wood rot that eventually attack all outdoor furniture.

To solve the problem, first decide how important it is to you to hide the holes entirely. If you do not mind the sight of the countersunk openings, simply carry on with your finishing. If you paint, fill the holes with the first coat of sealer/primer you apply. If you stain, fill the holes with that; the little pools you create will soak into the surrounding wood and provide protection, and some will remain to dry and partially fill the holes, covering the screwheads. If that does not seem like sufficient protection, carefully melt two or three drops of paraffin into each hole after you have completed your staining. The summer heat will ensure that each year, the paraffin will soften and settle into the holes, never working loose.

If you desire a more polished approach, you can use a wood filler to plug the holes entirely before you apply your finish. Hardware stores sell several kinds of fillers, ranging from the plastic-wood varieties, which look and smell like sawdust stirred into model-airplane glue, and latex varieties, which look like vanilla pudding, to several new water-based materials that have the appearance of wet belt-sander dust. All of these materials fill holes perfectly well. But keep a few things in mind:

Fill large holes in two or more stages to prevent the material from cracking.

Overfill the holes, because most fillers shrink when they dry.

Some fillers will not accept some finishes, especially stains. This is an exasperating limitation, and you won't discover it until a guest sitting in the chair you completed last weekend stands up with a little row of stain buttons attached to the back of her sweatshirt. Test each finish with each filler.

Even if you do not plan to apply any finish, test every wood filler. Some brands react with the resins in such woods as cedar to produce a dark blotch around the hole you have filled. That, too, shows up only after a couple of days, so do your tests well ahead of time.

You will notice, if you read the labels on paint cans, that instructions for priming raw wood always insist that you apply your first coat **before** you use caulking or wood fillers. My friend Jeff explained this to me: "The practice of applying the first coat of primer before the putty or caulk or wood fill originated in the days when such items were largely oil-based. The raw wood fibres sucked out the oil almost instantly, so the putty tended to crack and fall out of the hole before the primer went on. Since early paints were oil-based, they had the same greasiness as early putty, and the two dried out at about the same rate."

Conventional wisdom today still says primer before putty, partly from tradition and partly because you don't want anything between the wood and the prime coat. All of which is to say that priming before filling ensures not only that filler cures slowly and well but also that if the wood filler does work loose and fall out, the wood will remain protected. But do not forget to apply a primer coat to the dried wood filler itself before the finish coat goes on to ensure a uniform final surface.

# CUTTING DIAGRAM AND MATERIALS LIST

## MATERIALS LIST

one 10-foot ⁵⁄₄x8
one 10-foot ⁵⁄₄x4
one 8-foot ⁵⁄₄x4
five 6-foot ⁵⁄₄x8s
eight small blocks from scrap

1¾" #8 wood screws
2½" #8 wood screws
waterproof glue

## PARTS LIST

| | |
|---|---|
| 4 leg pieces | ⁵⁄₄x4"x29" |
| 4 leg pieces | ⁵⁄₄x3"x29" |
| 2 side aprons | ⁵⁄₄x4x56" |
| 2 end aprons | ⁵⁄₄x4x29½" |
| 1 stringer | ⁵⁄₄x4x29½" |
| 5 top boards | ⁵⁄₄x8x60" |
| 8 small blocks | |

## CUTTING DIAGRAM

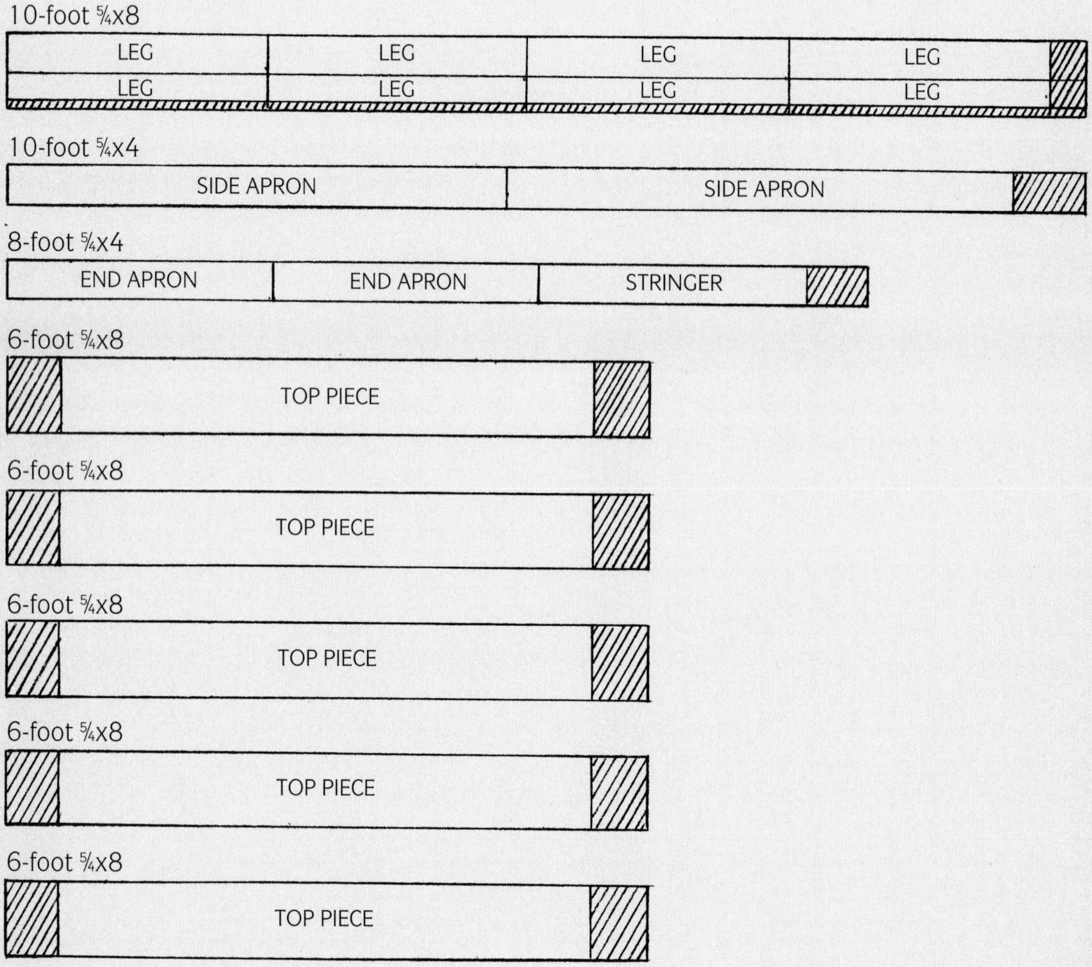

10-foot ⁵⁄₄x8

| LEG | LEG | LEG | LEG | |
|---|---|---|---|---|
| LEG | LEG | LEG | LEG | |

10-foot ⁵⁄₄x4

| SIDE APRON | SIDE APRON | |
|---|---|---|

8-foot ⁵⁄₄x4

| END APRON | END APRON | STRINGER | |
|---|---|---|---|

6-foot ⁵⁄₄x8

| | TOP PIECE | |
|---|---|---|

6-foot ⁵⁄₄x8

| | TOP PIECE | |
|---|---|---|

6-foot ⁵⁄₄x8

| | TOP PIECE | |
|---|---|---|

6-foot ⁵⁄₄x8

| | TOP PIECE | |
|---|---|---|

6-foot ⁵⁄₄x8

| | TOP PIECE | |
|---|---|---|

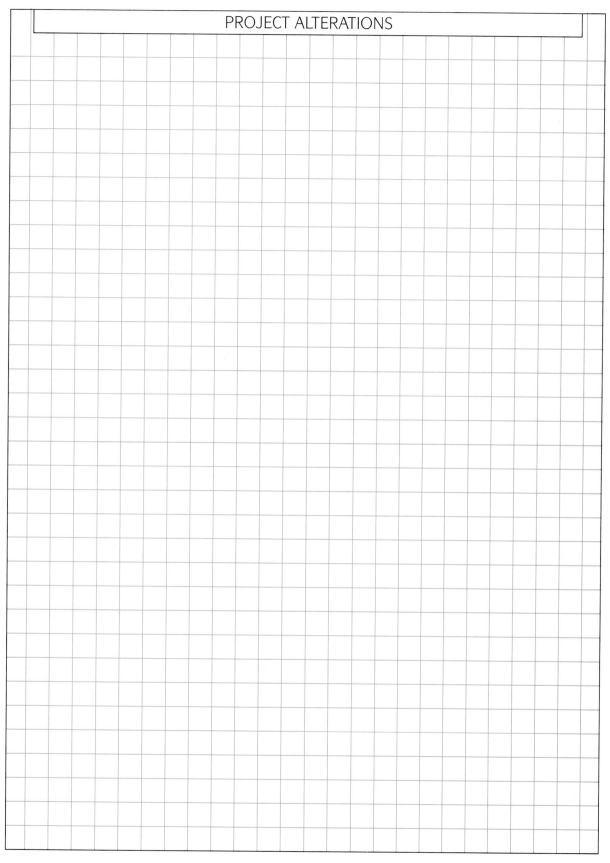

# PROJECT ALTERATIONS

A friend watching me scratch my head over chair design commented, "They say if you can build a chair, you can build anything." It was meant to be a compliment. I think it was meant to be encouraging too. But it is not clear what comfort to take from the old saw, since, strictly speaking, it means if you can't build everything, then you can't build a chair.

No doubt about it, chairs are difficult. A chair, after all, is nothing but a set of levers waiting to rip itself apart. When a person leans back in a chair and tips it onto its hind legs, the seat itself becomes a prybar inserted into the back support; the farther out on the seat the bum rests, the greater the leverage acting on the joints. If your 180-pound brother-in-law tips back your handmade deck chair and then gets most of his weight balanced out on the front

edge of the 18-inch seat, he is exerting thousands of pounds of force on whatever joint you've used to assemble the thing. He and the chair are likely to collapse at any second.

For people who don't tip back but prefer to wiggle around a lot, there is the possibility that their seat will crumple sideways just as aluminum chairs with metal fatigue inevitably settle in the wrong direction. In fact, the more you know about chairs, the more it seems a miracle that they work at all and the less likely you are to feel confident about building them. On the other hand, understanding how chairs go together adds a certain excitement to just lounging around with friends.

Just as with tables and benches, the perfectly strong chair would be a solid block. If you begin with the ideal of a back support cut into a

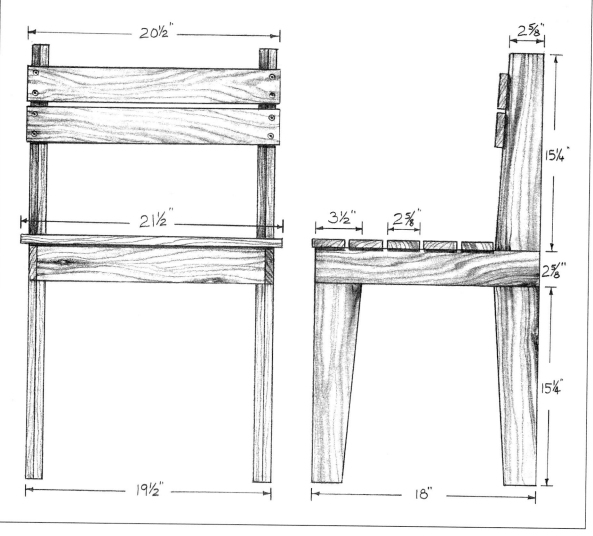

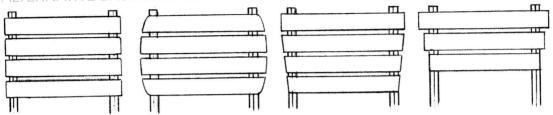

stump, every other design is a compromise that trades away strength to limit weight, save on materials or produce an aesthetically pleasing shape. Very careful joinery makes it all possible, and that is why chair making is held in such high esteem. If you can make a chair, well, you've accomplished something.

The design below provides for those outdoor occasions that require something more formal-looking than a bench at the table. The flexibility of the design allows you to modify it to suit the ensemble. It is lightweight but sturdy, and when glued together with resorcinol or epoxy glue, it can be left outside if it must be. It requires no joinery, because although the secret to most chairs is some version of the mortise-and-tenon joint, in this case, you replace meticulous joints with carefully glued subassemblies.

Read the instructions before you decide on the shape of the leg supports and the height and look of the back—you can customize your own style. Once you have decided on the final appearance, lay out the pieces, mix up the glue, and begin piecing things together.

## TWO NOTES

In this chair, the seat slats, backrests, legs and aprons are all made of 1x3 cedar. The material can be purchased from a building-supply yard, but since the smaller dimensions often get sawed from the roughest wood, sometimes better-quality material can be had by buying 1x6 and ripping it in half to produce pieces with a finished width of 2⅝ inches. *Your decision will determine the exact lengths of some pieces.*

For the notches required in this plan and for the spacing of the gap in the rear leg assembly, do not use a tape measure; instead, hold up a piece of the actual wood you are working with in order to trace out cutting lines.

1 Begin with the backs. In most chair designs, the rear legs extend well above the seat to support the backrest. In this design, the leg/back assembly consists of three pieces of wood glued together. The main member stretches from the top of the back to the foot of the leg and is simply a straight 1x3. The other two pieces can be whatever size and shape suit your taste.

The prototype chair for this book has tapers on both the leg and the backrest, with each piece flared from the width of a 1x3 out to 3½ (the full width of a 1x4). A more intricate shape, however, is just as appropriate, and in all cases, the simplest way to proceed is to cut the two side pieces to their proper length before adding a taper or design.

## LEG/BACK ASSEMBLY

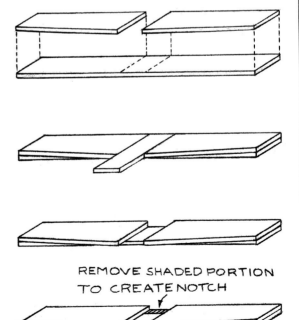

REMOVE SHADED PORTION TO CREATE NOTCH

2 Glue each set of leg and back pieces together so that the space left between the tapered pieces is exactly the width of the chair's side apron. (See illustration #1, facing page.) If you are careful not to let any glue leak into the wrong gap, you can clamp the side apron into its place while the glue is setting to ensure the spacing (illustration #2). Tighten the joint with a line of #6 1¼-inch wood screws down the centre of the 1x3, then set the two rear assemblies aside overnight (illustration #3).

3 When they have set, cut a notch for the back apron in the back edge of each assembly where the wood is only one layer thick. The notch should be exactly the same width as the space in the glued-up assemblies and as deep as the thickness of the wood you are using (approximately ¾ inch). Check everything carefully. Each finished assembly should look like illustration #4, facing page. The distance from the bottom of each assembly to the top of the notch should be 17⅞ inches or so depending on the true width of the 1x3 material you are using. This distance determines the exact length of the 1x3 front leg members that you use in the next step.

4 The front legs are similar but less complicated. Here again, a piece of 1x3 attaches to a shorter member; this time, the shorter piece is simply a support. Once again, use resorcinol or epoxy glue to attach the

two pieces, and add a row of #6 1¼-inch screws. Clamp and set aside. Just as in the back legs, cut an additional notch in the 1x3 to accommodate the front apron. The illustration (bottom left) shows the notch in the 1x3 leg member. Note that the top corner has been cut off at an angle so that rainwater dripping from the gap in the slats above does not collect on the end grain.

## CHAIR ASSEMBLY

*The manner in which the chair back and seat are assembled takes the place of a mortise-and-tenon joint, the joint that does most of the work in standard chair designs. The assembly does far more than simply support the seat from below. It allows a person to tilt this chair onto its hind legs without immediately ripping everything apart. The side apron is like a lever with its fulcrum at the front edge of the leg support. When the chair is tipped back, the short attached back piece is the immovable object that deals with the irresistible force of that lever.*

FRONT LEG DETAIL

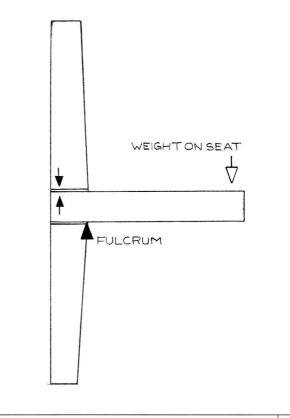

WEIGHT ON SEAT

FULCRUM

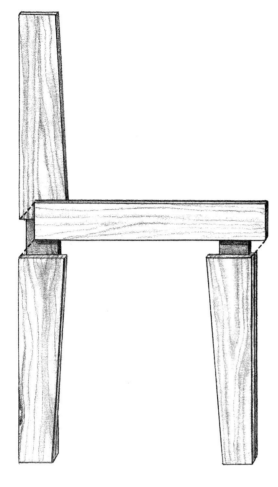

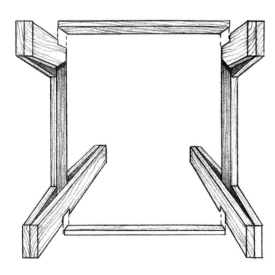

5 After the legs are glued and set, attach them together to form the two side assemblies (each made up of a back leg, the corresponding front leg and the connecting side apron), once again using glue and screws and clamps. The side apron extends from the front of the front leg to the back of the back leg. Make sure that the top of the apron and the front of the front leg are at 90 degrees to each other and that the top of the apron and the back of the back leg are also at 90 degrees. (See illustration.) As well, make sure that the two side assemblies are exact mirror images. In theory, this is redundant; in practice, it is a very good idea. You can even lay one on top of the other as you are gluing and clamping them together, but be sure to separate them with a layer of wax paper or plastic so that you don't end up gluing them together.

6 Join the side assemblies by installing the front and back aprons. These fit into the notches cut in the 1x3 member of the legs and should butt tightly against the side aprons. As you are doing this, tighten everything in place with bar clamps, taking extreme care that the side assemblies remain perfectly parallel to each other and that the tops and bottoms of the legs stay in line. You can check this by measuring from the top corner of the right front leg to the bottom corner of the left front leg and then measuring from the top corner of the left front leg to the bottom of the right front leg. These two diagonals must be absolutely equal. In theory, the only screws and nails you need for this chair are the wood screws holding the slats in place. In practice, however, as you assemble everything, you may find yourself reaching for some #6 1¼-inch wood screws and the occasional finishing nail. There is nothing wrong with that, and the heads of either screws or nails can be sunk right out of sight.

When you are confident that everything is square, set the completed chair frame aside until everything sets. Once the glue hardens, this chair will possess remarkable rigidity, but until then, it will try to slump over under its own weight and under the weight of the clamps. So arrange everything carefully on a flat surface, and tack braces in place if you think they are necessary.

## HOMEMADE CLAMPS AND PRESSES

*In place of joints cut into solid wood, the chair plans rely on assembling the various parts from flat stock and then fitting those together into a final form. This requires gluing, and that requires clamps. Here are plans for custom clamps that suit this project perfectly.*

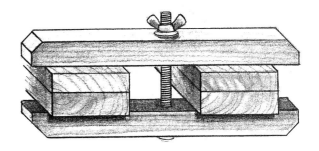

*The secret to fitting the clamps to a particular task lies in cutting the heel (the pivot point at the far end of the clamp) to a length that equals the thickness of the pieces to be held in the jaws: if you plan to glue two pieces of wood ¾ inch thick, cut the heel so that it measures 1½ inches at its longest point.*

*You can even create a small press for gluing the pieces of this chair by leaving your clamp open on both ends. With the carriage bolt at the centre of two open jaws, you can fit materials to be clamped into each end, and as long as they are the same thickness, the jaws will tighten down evenly.*

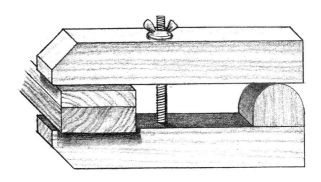

*All you need to make your own clamps and presses are some ⅜-inch carriage bolts of 5 or 6 inches, some washers and wing nuts and hardwood that can be cut to approximately 1 by 1½ inches by 6 or 7 inches.*

7 With the four legs, the four aprons and the two back uprights now in place, all that remains is to install the seat slats and two more slats for the backrest with #6 1¾-inch wood screws. Five 1x3 slats with a space of approximately ⅜ inch between them cover the seat nicely. Take care that the front slat does not overhang the front apron by more than ¼ inch, or it will split. The position of the backrest is entirely a matter of taste, but it should come somewhere between 8 inches and 14 inches above the seat.

## MODIFICATIONS

Not only the backrests, but everything about this chair is very adaptable, once you understand the basic elements. Before you begin building, you should decide how you want it to look and feel and work.

This chair can be made wider or narrower or deeper or shallower from front to back without changing anything in the design or construction except the length of the appropriate aprons and slats.

As well, you may want to adopt one of the Shakers' ideas and cut the back down far enough that the whole chair fits under the table you plan to use. The Shaker low-back chair was designed so that while it still provided support for the sitter, it could be shoved right out of sight when it wasn't in use. Outdoors, having easy storage and protection for the chairs is a boon, and this idea works especially well with trestle tables, since they have no apron.

The seat slats can be lengthened and then cut to a gentle curve on either side, as can the back.

Finally, most chairs have a slope to the seat and a corresponding slope to the back (the Adirondack chair is the extreme of this), and these particular chairs can be given a more relaxed posture by simply cutting the bottom of the legs at a consistent shallow angle and tipping everything slightly to the rear. To mark that line, place the front legs up on, say, blocks of half-inch plywood, then lay a length of 1-inch material alongside the front and back legs to trace one straight line.

## MATERIALS LIST

one 8-foot 1x4
two 8-foot 1x6s

1¼" #6 wood screws
1¾" #6 wood screws
1¼" finishing nails
waterproof glue

## PARTS LIST

| | |
|---|---|
| 5 seat slats | 1x3x21½" |
| 2 back slats | 1x3x20½" |
| 2 back support members | 1x4x15¼" |
| 4 leg members | 1x4x15¼" |
| 2 front leg members | 1x3x18" |
| 4 aprons | 1x3x18" |
| 2 back support/leg members | 1x3x32" |

## CUTTING DIAGRAM

8-foot 1x4

| BACK SUPPORT | BACK SUPPORT | LEG MEMBER | LEG MEMBER | LEG MEMBER | LEG MEMBER | |

8-foot 1x6 ripped in half

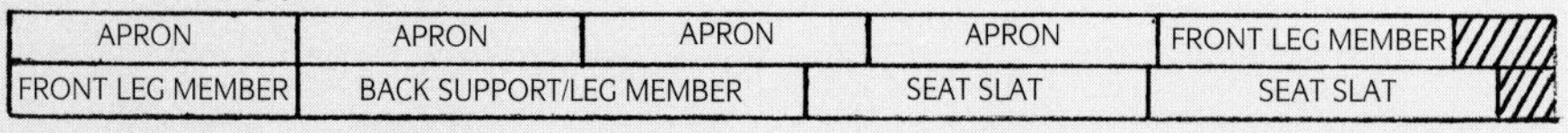

| APRON | APRON | APRON | APRON | FRONT LEG MEMBER | |
| FRONT LEG MEMBER | BACK SUPPORT/LEG MEMBER | | SEAT SLAT | SEAT SLAT | |

8-foot 1x6 ripped in half

| BACK SUPPORT/LEG MEMBER | BACK SLAT | BACK SLAT | SEAT SLAT | |
| SEAT SLAT | SEAT SLAT | | | |

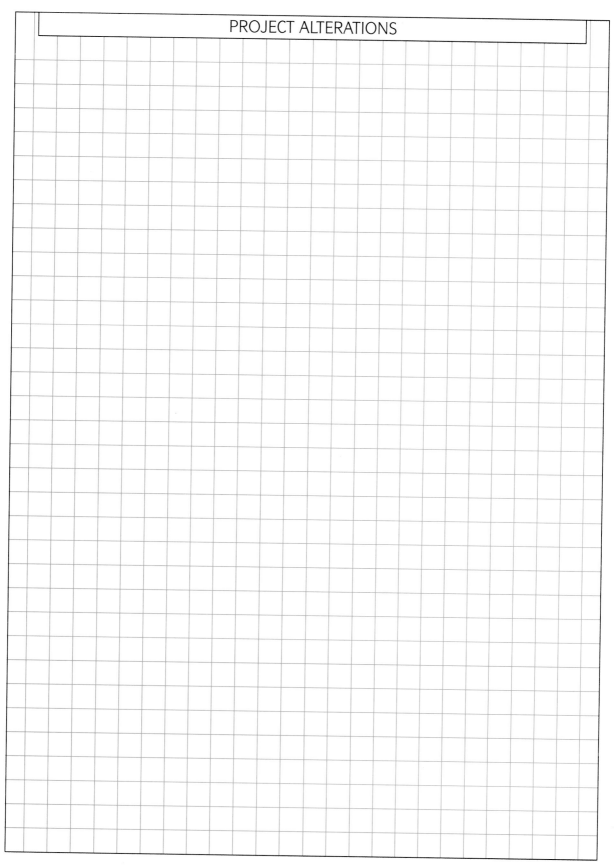

The trestle table is like a riddle that you can set for dinner: it has four feet but only two legs. In many ways, it is simply a large bench with a broad area on each end to support the top and a wide stance on the ground. But since a 30-inch-high bench would be an overwhelmingly bulky piece of work, furniture makers have traditionally made allowances. In place of wide planks at each end, for example, trestle tables make the most of a pair of narrow uprights.

To understand how a trestle works, imagine assembling a cheap and nasty table from four pieces of plywood. Three identical pieces are set on edge to form an H shape when viewed from above. The fourth piece sits on top. Even fastened together with a few screws into the end grain of the plywood, such a table would be impressively sturdy. The two parallel end pieces would prevent the table from tipping from side to side, and the stretcher between them would make it impossible for the table to rack. Now imagine cutting away as much of those pieces of

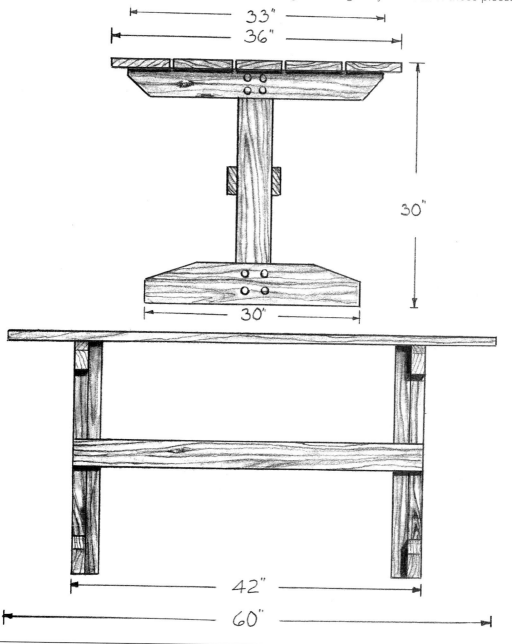

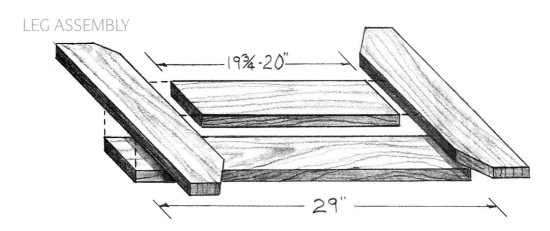

plywood as possible without letting everything fall over—that's how a trestle table works.

A fixed trestle table consists of 15 lengths of plank glued and screwed or bolted together. Begin by cutting everything to length, including the taper on both the feet and the arms. You can adjust the amount of taper to suit your taste, but the arms should have some upward sweep to them, and the legs should narrow toward the ends. These angled cuts have more to do with how the table looks than anything else, but they also serve to minimize the amount of material projecting into the space where people put their legs.

Now chamfer every edge of every single piece of wood. This sounds like an odd instruction, but it works well on the theory that if you can't prevent gaps showing between the planks that you have butted together, then make those potential gaps into an aesthetic statement. You want to emphasize the fact that this trestle table is assembled from lumber rather than a solid hunk of wood. Set aside the pieces you have cut for the top; you won't need them until the last minute, and you will need all the available space in your workshop to work on the leg assemblies.

1 Apply plenty of waterproof glue, then fix the feet and arms to the *longer* leg pieces using a couple of clamps or even some finishing nails. Drill ¼-inch holes, four for each foot and arm, so that you can bolt everything together. Tighten it all down with carriage bolts or hex bolts and T-nuts, making sure that the heads of the bolts show on the outside; that is, on the horizontal feet and arm pieces.

2 You should now have two large I's. Be sure that all the angles are 90 degrees, then double-check the gap between the tops and bottoms. Cut the shorter leg pieces to fit into those spaces, then spread glue on one whole side and on the ends before setting them in place. If you have to drive each into place using a hammer and a block of wood, all the better, within reason, of course. Screw the two leg pieces together using #8 2½-inch wood screws installed from the *inside* of the leg where the nuts are located, the side that won't show.

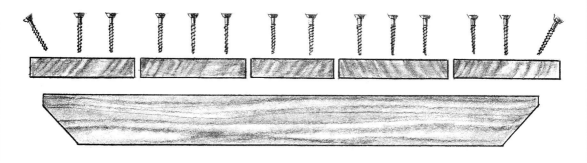

The second leg piece, in addition to helping carry the load from above, acts as a brace that prevents the arms and feet from rocking back and forth. Attached with only bolts and then subjected to years of people leaning on it, the arms would eventually work loose, creating a teeter-totter top.

3 Stand the leg assemblies upright, approximately 36 to 37 inches apart, and picture how the stringers will be positioned. The bottom of each stringer should be about 16 inches off the ground. Mark that point, then tip the leg assemblies on their sides and position a stringer, making sure that it rests at 90 degrees to the legs.

Carefully mark the stringer for the two predrilled ⅛-inch holes you will need at each end for the lag screws. Drill one hole into the outside 2x6 leg member and the other hole into the inside leg member. When you flip the assembly over to mark the other stringer, reverse the position of the holes so that you don't end up trying to put two screws into the same place.

Spread plenty of waterproof glue and attach the stringers to the legs with ¼-by-3-inch lag screws. (Note: Having positioned the stringers, you can cut notches for them and thereby gain additional stability. Consult "Cutting Notches," page 26.) Make one last check that all angles are at 90 degrees, and measure the diagonals just to be sure everything is still square. While you are at it, measure from each foot up to the top of the opposite arm as well. When it all checks out, gently put the frame aside on the flattest section of floor you have, and let the glue set. If the floor is crooked, the finished table will rock—assuming, of course, that your deck or patio is flat.

4 When the leg assemblies have dried, all that remains is to attach the top. As with the other tables described in this book, it is a good idea to groove the bottom of the tabletop planks to discourage warping. (See "Milling Grooves," page 60.) Then space the planks evenly so that the edge pieces overhang the arms by half an inch or so. The precise width of the gap between the pieces will vary with the lumber you purchase, but the spaces should be just under ½ inch. Predrill and countersink three holes in each end of the 8-inch boards

## CHAMFERING

*An arris, as my friend Jeff loves to tell the uninitiated, is a sharp angle formed by the intersection of two geometric planes. In other words, it is the 90-degree edge where, for example, the 2-inch side of a 2x4 meets the 4-inch side of the same 2x4. Not many people know what arrises are. Most of those who do are woodworkers.*

*Chamfering, a word whose meaning has remained unchanged since the 1500s, is the act of using a tool—nowadays most often a block plane or a small hand cutter that looks something like a bottle opener—to pare away that sharp-cornered arris and replace it with a third narrow plane, a bevelled edge or a chamfer.*

*When two planks with chamfered edges are butted together, the two bevels form a V, which in the case of the trestle table provides a nice detail. Chamfers on all the jointed surfaces cleverly disguise any irregularities in the cuts you make and any gaps that open between surfaces that you have glued.*

and two holes in each end of the 6-inch board, then spread more glue and screw them down to the arms using #8 2½-inch wood screws. If you have cut a steep taper on the arms, take care with the screws at the edge of outside planks; predrill the holes at a bit of an angle to avoid splitting the arm.

## FINAL NOTE

The weakness in this design is the point at which the stringers attach to the legs. Unless you cut notches, instead of wood bearing on wood, only the lag screws hold things together. With time, the table may begin to rock slightly from end to end. This can be forestalled by adding small triangular braces to attach the centre plank of the tabletop to the leg at each end. Predrill holes in the braces, and fix them in place with glue and wood screws.

If your table sees extremely hard use, you may later want to beef up these supports by adding another pair of braces that extend from the tops of the stringers to the sides of the legs.

## MATERIALS LIST

two 10-foot ⁵⁄₄x8s
one 6-foot ⁵⁄₄x6
one 8-foot 2x6
one 6-foot 2x6
one 6-foot 2x4
one 8-foot ⁵⁄₄x4

eight ¼"x3" lag screws
sixteen ¼"x3½" carriage bolts
2½" #8 wood screws
waterproof glue

## PARTS LIST

| | |
|---|---|
| 4 top boards | ⁵⁄₄x8x5' |
| 1 top board | ⁵⁄₄x6x5' |
| 2 leg pieces | 2x6x29" |
| 2 leg pieces | 2x6x20" (approx.) |
| 2 feet | 2x6x30" |
| 2 arms | 2x4x33" |
| 2 stringers | ⁵⁄₄x4x42" |

## CUTTING DIAGRAM

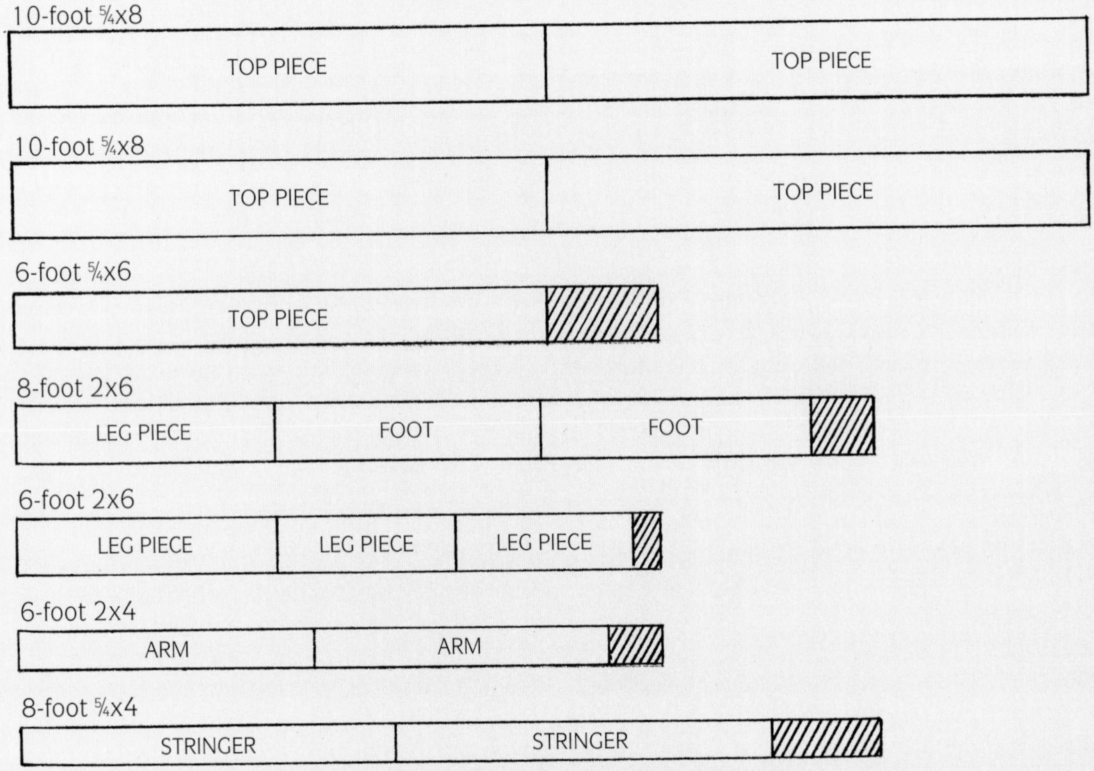

10-foot ⁵⁄₄x8

| TOP PIECE | TOP PIECE |
|---|---|

10-foot ⁵⁄₄x8

| TOP PIECE | TOP PIECE |
|---|---|

6-foot ⁵⁄₄x6

| TOP PIECE | |
|---|---|

8-foot 2x6

| LEG PIECE | FOOT | FOOT | |
|---|---|---|---|

6-foot 2x6

| LEG PIECE | LEG PIECE | LEG PIECE | |
|---|---|---|---|

6-foot 2x4

| ARM | ARM | |
|---|---|---|

8-foot ⁵⁄₄x4

| STRINGER | STRINGER | |
|---|---|---|

Light and spacious, trestle tables look good, and they offer extra room under the tabletop, where most tables are cluttered up with legs and the apron assembly that joins them together. In addition, trestle tables can be designed to do something most other tables cannot: come apart to save space. The plans that follow describe a trestle table that can be dismantled for easy winter storage.

As with several other projects in this book, the trestle table relies on a joint that is built instead of cut. Rather than drilling and chiselling a true mortise through the legs of the trestle, assemble each leg by sandwiching a pair of shorter ¾-inch boards between two lengths of 2-inch material and leaving a hole (the mortise) for the tongue you cut on each end of the stringer (the tenon) to pass through. The mortised leg possesses good durability, both because laminated wood is always stronger than a solid chunk and because assembled material does not suffer the same degree of warping, twisting and checking that larger dimensions of wood do.

This plan takes patience, but once you finish the table, the advantage of being able to break it down into pieces for transportation or storage can help you forget the glue-dripping, 4½-handed confusion that the project entails.

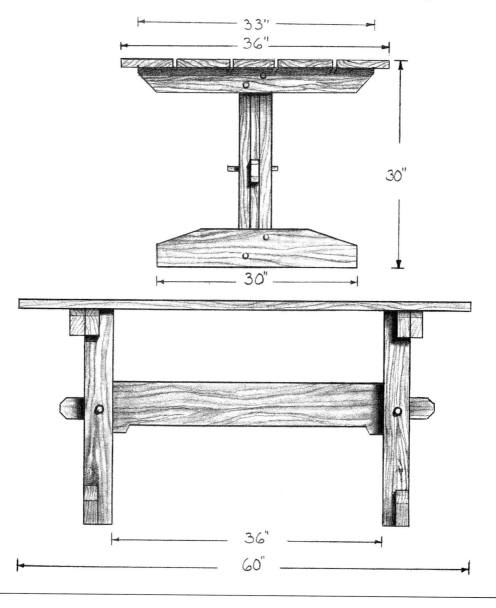

1 Begin by cutting all the pieces of wood to length *except the bottom pieces of ¾-inch material in the legs*. Do not trim those to final length; an extra fraction of an inch may serve you well when you assemble the legs.

2 Assemble the stringer first because, while it is not the most complicated piece in the table, you do have to cut large tenons on either end of it, and if you establish their precise dimensions now, you can make the mortises you build in the legs fit them *exactly*.

Lay out the tenons carefully, keeping in mind that the shoulders of each tenon, where the stringer will bear against the table leg, must be cut perfectly square and in line. If you cut the shoulder above the tenon even a hair out of line with the shoulder below the tenon, you will build a wobble into your table.

3 Now set out the materials for the legs—including the two ¾-inch pieces that you left a bit too long—and arm yourself with glue and a fistful of 3½-inch finishing nails. Use plastic resin glue or an alternative that cleans up easily, rather than epoxy or resorcinol.

At each end, assemble the three exact-cut pieces with glue and nails to tack everything together, with the ¾-inch piece sandwiched between the two 2-inch pieces. Then slip the stringer into place so that the tenons on the ends of the stringer fill the precise spot where you want to locate the finished mortise. Only when the stringer is thus properly positioned and square to both legs should you fit the last two pieces of ¾-inch material into the remaining gaps between the 2-inch pieces and snugly up against the tenons. Glue will be squishing out everywhere, and about now, you will be very upset if you ignored the advice about not using epoxy.

Nail everything together, then immediately slide the stringer back out of the mortise.

## LEG ASSEMBLY

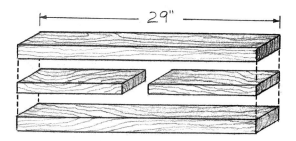

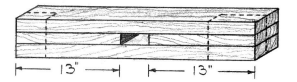

Use your battered renovating chisel or a narrow putty knife to clean away the gobs of glue still oozing from the cracks *inside* the mortise, and wipe off the stringer.

Now trim the extra wood from the bottom centre piece of ¾-inch material. Use a nail set to drive the heads of the finishing nails into the wood, and tighten everything down with clamps while the glue sets. (If you prefer, you can snug everything up with some countersunk #8 3-inch wood screws, but you should still let the glue set before carrying on.)

4 Measure the precise dimension of the 2x4s and 2x6s selected for the arms and feet of the end assemblies, transfer those measurements to the legs, and cut the necessary notches. Cut carefully so that all the gluing surfaces meet precisely. Position the arms and feet in the notches, and predrill ¼-inch holes. Spread glue on both faces of each notch, and attach the arms and feet with ¼-by-4-inch carriage bolts. Be sure that the arms and feet are set at exactly 90 degrees to the legs before putting the completed assemblies aside to set.

## STRINGER

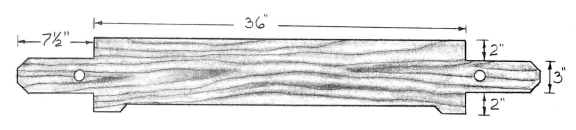

## CROSSCUTS WITH A RAFTER SQUARE

Circular saws belong on a construction site, where framers use them to sort out the sizes of various 2-inch stock. For that reason, using one in the shop can feel a little like trying to use a combine in the garden—it has far too much power for the jobs at hand, and it lacks subtlety. More to the point, it doesn't cut in straight lines but in close approximations. The problems show up when you try to piece together the approximately straight edges of your furniture pieces.

This is one of those tricks that everyone who owns a speed square eventually figures out. Also known as an American rafter square, a speed square is a cast-aluminum right-angle triangle with a lip running along one of the sides that is not the hypotenuse. It comes with a booklet of instructions, which addresses those worthy people who want to lay out their own rafters instead of buying space-wasting trusses. But the square itself is perfect simplicity. Rafters and stud walls aside, it can transform your circular saw from a growling implement of rough construction into something that vaguely resembles a precision tool.

Hook the lip of the square over the far side of the material you want to mark, and trace either the 90-degree or 45-degree line with your pencil. Then slide the square along the workpiece far enough that when you line up the blade of your circular saw with the line you've made, the base of the saw fits right along the edge of the square. The beauty of the heavy aluminum design is that the same edges you trace along are also thick enough to safely guide the base of your saw, and if you now hold everything firmly, the square will force the blade to travel a true line. The triangular shape of the square makes it easy to grip with the same hand you are using to steady the workpiece.

If you go looking for a speed square, find one that has ground edges. You will be able to spot the difference: cheaper models still show the slight imperfections produced by the casting process. The good ones have been finished with an accurate edge so sharp that you can cut yourself.

5 Now come the most careful moments of the entire project. The rigidity of the assembled table relies entirely on a tight connection between the stringer and the end assemblies: the shoulders of the tenons you cut on the stringer must not only line up accurately with the wood surrounding the mortise you built, they must be pulled into taut contact with the legs.

A dowel holds everything together at each end, and you place the whole arrangement under tension by cutting the various holes for the dowels slightly out of alignment. In order for each dowel to get through a hole in one side of the leg, then through a second hole in the stringer, then out through a third hole in the other side of the leg, it should have to drag each tenon a fraction of an inch tighter into its mortise than it actually wants to go.

To arrange the holes, first mark the exact centre of the mortise on both sides of each leg (use a combination square to transfer the location of the mortise around to the sides of the legs, then trace the diagonals to mark the centre points). Drill ⅛-inch guide holes straight through from those centre points. Assemble the legs and stringer, and while holding them tightly together, push a scratch awl or a nail into the guide holes to transfer the location of that centring hole onto the tenons of the stringer. Disassemble everything again.

Now, unless you own a drill press, use a hole

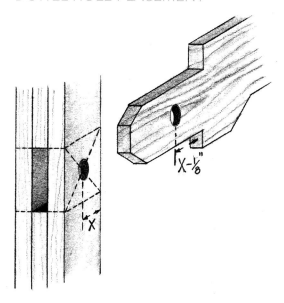

saw rather than a drill bit to enlarge the holes in the legs to the 1¼-inch diameter of the dowel. A hole saw is a small drill bit with a large collar made up of concentric circles into which you fit cutters, each of which looks like a coarse hacksaw blade bent into a circle. A large bit in a hand-held drill usually makes a mess of softwood, but the hole saw will remove a lovely cylinder of material into which the dowel should fit perfectly.

Locate the marks you made on the tenons, then relocate them ⅛ inch or less closer to the shoulder of the tenons—away from the ends of the stringer. Drill guide holes, and use your hole saw to enlarge these as well.

Now, when you reassemble the ends and the stringer, all the holes should almost line up, but not quite. Bevel the dowels so that they look a

bit like sharpened pencils, and carefully but firmly drive them through the holes. They should pull things together so tightly that nothing wiggles. It should, in fact, be almost magical how sturdy it suddenly all becomes.

6 Although the top of this table is a separate structure that can be removed, the easiest way to build it involves bolting the crosspieces for the top directly to the arms of the leg assembly. Predrill the holes for two bolts at each end, and use 4-inch bolts.

Note: You will notice that the heads of the carriage bolts connecting the arms to the legs get in the way of the crosspieces you are trying to install. Either remove the carriage bolts long enough to countersink a hole for the heads (which you will be able to do since the glue will hold everything steady), or, with a softwood such as pine, use the crude but effective expedient of simply tightening the nuts until the heads sink themselves flush with the surface.

Before you tighten the bolts connecting the arms and the crosspieces, lay a length of wax paper over the tops of the *arms* and also tuck it between the arms and the crosspieces that you will be connecting to the top boards. If you ignore this precaution, you will glue the top of the table to both sets of legs. Your knockdown trestle table will then be one solid, permanent piece of furniture, and all this fussing around with precise measurements will have been an elaborate waste of time.

Space out the top pieces, and attach them to the crosspieces just as described in the instructions for the permanent trestle table. Remember that cutting grooves in the underside of the top boards will forestall cupping and twisting. (See "Milling Grooves," page 60.)

# CUTTING DIAGRAM AND MATERIALS LIST

## MATERIALS LIST

two 10-foot 5/4x8s
one 6-foot 5/4x6
two 8-foot 2x4s
one 6-foot 2x6
one 6-foot 5/4x4
one 6-foot 2x4
one 6-foot 5/4x8

3½" finishing nails
3" #8 wood screws
2½" #8 wood screws
twelve ¼"x4" carriage bolts
waterproof glue

## PARTS LIST

| | |
|---|---|
| 4 top pieces | 5/4x8x5' |
| 1 top piece | 5/4x8x5' |
| 2 crosspieces | 2x4x33" |
| 2 arms | 2x4x33" |
| 4 leg pieces | 2x4x29" |
| 2 leg pieces | 5/4x4x13" |
| 2 leg pieces | 5/4x4x13½"* |
| 2 feet | 2x6x30" |
| 1 stringer | 5/4x8x51½" |
| 2 pegs | 1-1¼" diam. x6" |

*if all goes well, these pieces will be trimmed to 13" after assembly. See step 3.

## CUTTING DIAGRAM

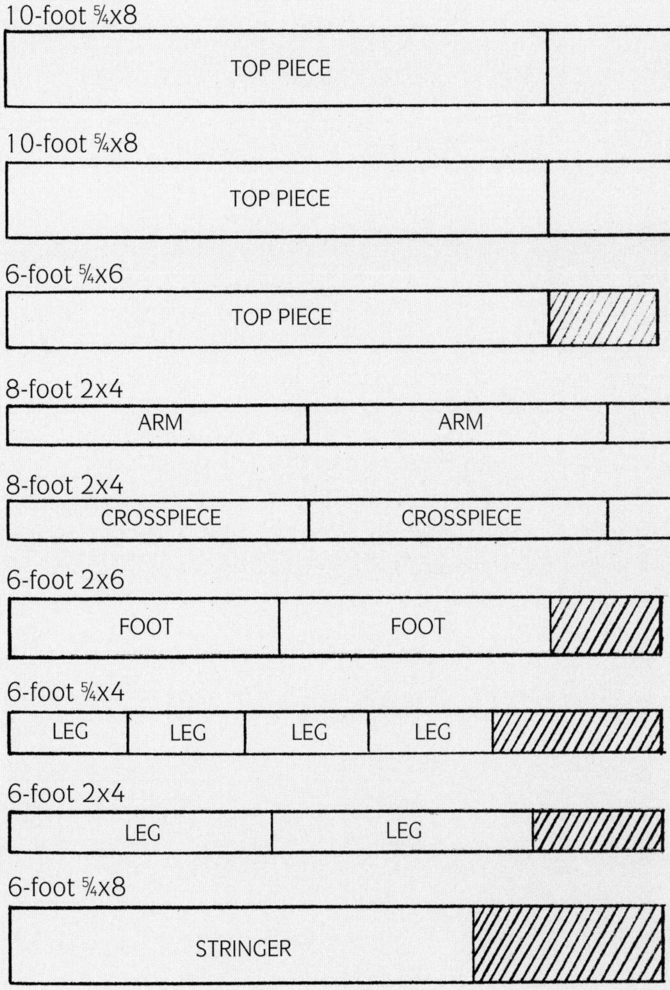
10-foot 5/4x8
TOP PIECE
TOP PIECE
10-foot 5/4x8
TOP PIECE
TOP PIECE
6-foot 5/4x6
TOP PIECE
8-foot 2x4
ARM
ARM
LEG
8-foot 2x4
CROSSPIECE
CROSSPIECE
LEG
6-foot 2x6
FOOT
FOOT
6-foot 5/4x4
LEG
LEG
LEG
LEG
6-foot 2x4
LEG
LEG
6-foot 5/4x8
STRINGER

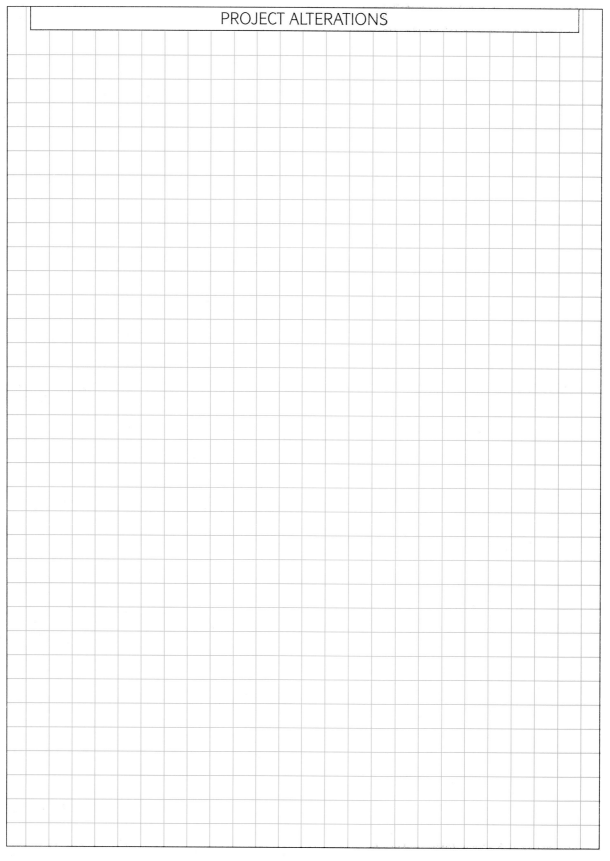

I hate Adirondack chairs. The only graceful way to get out of an Adirondack chair involves a modified version of what gymnasts call a kip: draw your knees way up, place your hands against the back of the chair on either side of the head, then vault directly into a standing position with a single back-arching flip of the body. If you can't accomplish that—and who can, really?—the alternative is to struggle from the seat by walking on the cheeks of your bum, clutching your empty beer glass, the way everyone else does.

The difficulty most people have with Adirondacks is a result of the fact that taller people need larger chairs. Most Adirondacks are designed to accommodate even big sitters. For that reason, they swallow almost everyone else whole, and they usually don't want to let go.

When you first slide down into an Adirondack, you experience for one brief instant the illusion of perfect comfort; that's the part everyone loves. But with your first fidget, that illusion disappears, never to return. Adirondacks are posture tyrants, forcing the user to sit in a single precise position: knees up and not too far apart, shoulders squared and held in place by the curving back, head straight, hips set firmly back into what I think of as the Adirondack bucket and arms resting out from the body, pointing straight ahead. And when you are finished thus reclining at attention, there comes the indignity of departure. Adirondacks can be awfully hard on your dignity.

History, however, has made the Adirondack synonymous with outdoor furniture. One can no more write about building outdoor chairs without mentioning the curved classic than one can describe the Paris skyline without mentioning the Eiffel Tower.

But I have an additional beef about Adirondack chairs that has to do with how I imagine the design evolved and how I think it can be rehabilitated. An Adirondack chair can be a very simple thing. The design exploits the principle that the human form sitting down fits into something roughly the shape of a Z lying on its side, a shape that happens to be relatively easy to construct.

The seat of an Adirondack forms the sloping part of the Z; the front legs and the back form

## WOOD AND WATER

*If you cut a block of wood from a freshly felled evergreen, put it in a vise and squeeze, water runs out in a steady stream. Each cell of the wood fibre originally formed part of a conduit that supported the living tree by lifting liquid from the roots to the needles. Only a powerful pump transports water as far from the ground as trees do, and cutting trunks into lumber does little to change the fact that, first and foremost, wood moves water.*

*Once a board is cut and dried, however, it never takes up as much water as it started with, unless someone submerges it in a lake and leaves it there for a good long time. Nevertheless, wood continues to react to the humidity of its surroundings. A furniture maker may transform the original plank entirely, but the most elaborate wooden chair, for all the careful shaping and gluing and fastening it has undergone, still remains a sponge, expanding and contracting with the moisture around it.*

*The best you can do is build your piece, seal all the top surfaces and wait for a string of hot summer days to dry out the wood completely. On one of those days, when it is too hot to do anything else, apply a coat of sealer to the bottoms.*

*The 1949* **Everybody's Home Fix-It Guide** *suggests that "if you cannot tell any other way, you can test your own wood for 'greenness' by weighing it when dry; then place it in a warm oven and allow it stand for some time, and weigh it over again. If the weight is considerably less, the wood is 'green.' " This is useful advice if the piece of furniture you plan to build is smaller than a pot roast. Otherwise, keep in mind that after a few weeks, wood stabilizes at roughly the humidity of its surroundings. If your shop is dry and the wood has been there for some time, the wood will be dry. If your shop is damp, the wood will be too, and so on. Wood is best worked at about 15 to 20 percent moisture content.*

*Understand, however, that no matter what you do, some distortion in the materials is likely. You may still have to make adjustments after your furniture has seen a summer of use and the legs don't all quite meet the floor anymore.*

the top and bottom, and the arms of the chair are simply braces you need to hold the Z steady. The whole thing should practically put itself together.

Unfortunately, the Adirondack long ago fell victim to the simplicity of its own design. Everyone could make them, so everyone did, and everyone had an opinion about improving things, to the point that some Adirondacks are now more embellishment than chair. I decided that if this book were to include Adirondacks, they would have to be basic units—Z chairs.

I'd never built an Adirondack chair, so I bought some plans from my favourite tool catalogue and invited a friend who had a different set of plans to join me in the shop. My plans, as it turned out, were for the Cadillac of lawn furniture. These were not chairs for the grass or the deck or even a folk-art museum; these were chairs for a gallery, complicated by an absurdity of curves. They were so improved that by the time I was through cutting out the parts, the scrap pile dwarfed my stack of slats and legs and braces. Our second set of plans was better but still reflected a long history of fiddling around.

We also repaired an admirably straightforward 25-year-old Adirondack that had rotted through in a few places and provided object lessons in the the physics of sitting down; the stress points were all easily identified by the clusters of nails and screws driven in by two or three generations of repairers. Finally, we reassembled another very simple Adirondack look-alike.

For weeks, we asked everyone who came into the shop to bum-test each of our five styles (the fancy plans included adjustments for either larger or smaller versions). Each of the chairs was someone's favourite, and none got significantly more votes than any of the others. Finally, we broke down the Adirondack to its essentials and built the simplest version we could imagine.

The plans below address several Adirondack problems. The arms are heavy and strong, because after I examined every Adirondack I could find, I discovered that the arms are always being busted and patched and renailed. I made the seat a single flat surface instead of the familiar curve because many people prefer the flat surface. Those who want the curve can add it. Similarly, the back consists of straight horizontal slats instead of a curving fan of verticals. Again, some prefer it that way, and you can make the modification yourself if you like. But more than anything, this design remains simple and can therefore be easily tailored to suit the people who will be using the chairs you build.

## CHAIR ANGLES

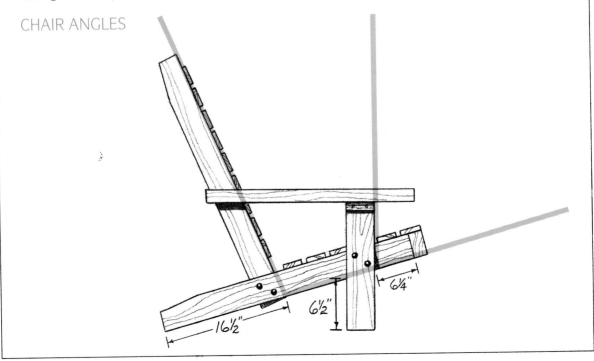

## BACK ADJUSTMENTS

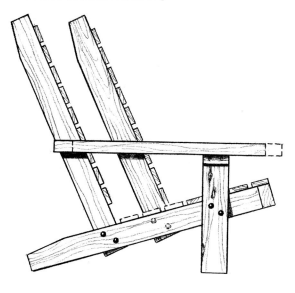

**1** Cut all materials to length, and before assembling the pieces, decide on the size and shape of the arms and how you want to decorate the back supports and the longer seat/leg members. You can leave them square or cut a simple bevel or round them off or cut an elaborate ogee shape, but this is the time to do it.

**2** Using a sliding T-bevel, transfer the angles traced across page 88 onto each set of legs. This is all the layout work that you should need to do. Give some thought to the location of your lines, however, because although the illustrations included here already give dimensions that will yield an average-sized chair, you can create a smaller or larger seat by moving the point at which the back intersects the seat/leg members. If your tiny great-aunt will be using the chair, locate the back closer to the front edge of the seat. If your hulking neighbour spends a great deal of time on your deck, provide him with a chair that is as long in the backside as he is (see illustration, above).

If you want a more specific method for customizing the chair, have the person who will be using it fill his or her pants' pockets with about $30 worth of pennies, then take a careful measurement from where the belt now hugs the top of the hips down to the fold at the back of the knees, and subtract approximately 6 inches—

more if there is a large curve to the backside in question. This represents the proper distance from the front of the seat to the front of the back supports. (When you are marking these lines, remember to allow for the 1½-inch-thick brace that crosses the front of the chair.)

As you mark the two seat/legs, keep in mind that they are a matched set, mirror images of each other. Mark the lines for the front legs on the outside of each seat/leg and the lines for the back supports on the insides.

**3** Line up the front legs with their mark on the seat/legs, and predrill holes so that you can then attach the pieces together using carriage bolts or hex bolts and T-nuts. Be sure to apply liberal dollops of glue. Compare the two side assemblies that you have now produced to ensure they are an exact match.

**4** Line up the back supports with their marks, and predrill and install them in the same manner as the front legs. Compare the two assemblies again, making sure they match.

## CROSS BRACES

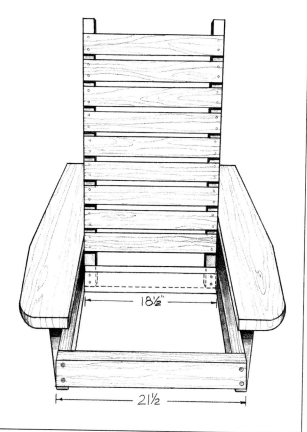

## ARM DETAIL

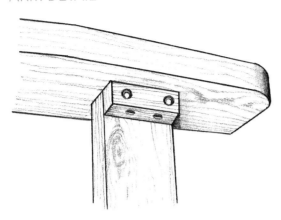

**5** Install the cross braces using #8 2½-inch wood screws and more glue. The longer cross brace attaches to the front of the seat/leg members, the shorter piece to the front edge of the back supports. Apply additional glue to the ends of the shorter cross brace so that they bond to the insides of the seat/leg members.

**6** Install the arms by setting them flat on the tops of the front legs and then marking their location on the back supports: the tops of the arms should be parallel to the floor. The point at which the arms meet the back will change with any changes you have made to customize the length of the seat, but there is enough length in the arms to accommodate substantial alterations.

The arms should reach to the back edge of the uprights. When you have them properly positioned, drill through the back supports, apply glue and attach the arms with the ⅜-inch lag screws driven into the arms themselves.

Do not attach the arms to the front legs until you have firmly connected the arms to the back supports. Before that connection is made, the exact position of each arm on each front leg is impossible to find, but after that connection is made, it is impossible to get it wrong.

Spread glue on the tops of the front legs, then drive a 4-inch finishing nail down through the arms to hold them in place. Predrill four holes through small 1x1x3½-inch blocks, and applying lots of glue, attach these at the junction of the arms and the front legs, driving two #8 2-inch screws up into the arms and two into the legs.

**7** Predrill two holes at each end of each slat, and beginning at the front edge of the seat, install the slats ¾ inch apart with #8 1¾-inch wood screws. Depending on whether you use 1x4 material or choose to rip 1x6-inch stock into narrower slats, there may be a gap where the seat intersects the back, but anything up to 5 inches is acceptable. On the backrest, you can set the top slat flush with the tops of the back supports or let the supports project slightly. To simplify installation, figure out where you want the top slat to end up, and then work up from the bottom; that way, you can rest a spare piece of stock on the previous slat as a spacer while you install the next one.

## ADDING CURVES

If you want to add a curved seat to these plans, simply substitute 2x6s for the 2x4s that form the seat/legs. After you have laid out the angles on these pieces as in Step 1 above, trace the curves you want onto the 2x6s and cut them out before assembly. A 4-litre paint can will give a good curve for the front edge of the seat, and a garbage-can lid will make an appropriate sweeping curve for the sunken portion of the seat.

The other modification you will have to make deals with the front cross brace. Shorten the 2x4 by 3 inches so that it fits between the seat/leg members, and install it as close to the

## CURVED SEAT

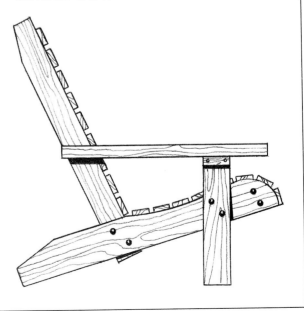

## THE NAMELESS DRILL TOOL

*Everything has a name; everything, that is, except my favourite little drill attachment. When you purchase one of these, it comes shrink-wrapped onto stiff backing that identifies it as a "slip-on drill tool," but that is no kind of name at all. It doesn't begin to tell you how smug you will feel every time you predrill holes for wood screws using your nameless gizmo and then slip it off to reveal the driver bit hidden inside.*

*The problem with using your drill as a power screwdriver is that even a moderately complex project requires you to open the chuck and exchange the countersink bit for the screw bit dozens of times, always when you are already holding the workpieces together with your left hand and your right knee and your chin. On such occasions, you will always have one remaining hand to*

*reach for the drill, but none to switch the bits. The slip-on tool, however, doesn't have to be tightened into the jaws of the drill. All you do is leave the Phillips or Robertson bit in your chuck, slide the countersink over the bit each time you need to drill a hole and slip it off again each time you need to drive a screw. The changeover can be managed with one hand.*

*The first time I saw someone stretch out a chalk line, I didn't understand what the string was for until it snapped down leaving a straight line. I was so charmed, it immediately became my idea of the perfect tool and has remained so ever since. The chucked countersink is almost as good, and unless you do professional layout for framing crews, you will use it far more often than you will your chalk line.*

front as you can without it interfering with the placement of seat slats on the curving front. Attach the cross brace with glue and #8 2½-inch wood screws driven through from the outside of the seat legs. You may also choose to cut some of the seat slats narrower so that they follow the curves more closely.

If you prefer the back of your chair to be formed by vertical slats instead of horizontals, assemble the front legs, seat and back piece as above. Then cut the back supports as shown in the illustration at right; install two 2x4 braces, one between the back supports, near the bottom, and the other over the top ends of the back supports. Attach vertical slats to the two new crosspieces you have added. If you use the same 1x6 material ripped in half, you should be able to fit five vertical slats in place. Finally, if you want the vertical slats to form a gentle curving embrace totally unlike any portion of the human body but more closely resembling the typical Adirondack, cut a very gentle curve into each of the two extra cross braces before you install them with #8 2½-inch wood screws and glue. When I say gentle, I mean an arc with a radius of 3 feet or more. If you make the curve any smaller, you will be forced to cut the vertical slats narrower to fit that inside contour.

To cut a rounded top on the vertical slats, you

can mark a perfect arc by tying one end of a string to your pencil. Hold the other end of the string somewhere along the centreline of the centre slat, and trace a mark onto the chair back. The longer the string, the gentler the curve.

## CURVED BACK

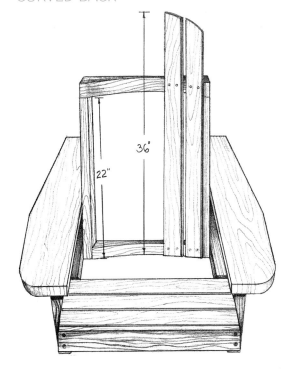

## MATERIALS LIST

one 8-foot 1x6
one 6-foot 1x6
one 6-foot 2x6
two 10-foot 2x4s
two small blocks from scrap 1x1x3½"

eight ⅜"x3½" carriage bolts
two ⅜"x2½" lag screws
2½" #8 wood screws
1¾" #8 wood screws
waterproof glue

## PARTS LIST

| | | |
|---|---|---|
| 9 back slats | 1x3x18½" |
| 6-7 seat slats | 1x3x21½" |
| 2 back supports | 2x4x36" |
| 2 seat supports | 2x4x36" |
| 2 front legs | 2x4x16¾" |
| 1 front cross brace | 2x4x21½" |
| 1 back cross brace | 2x4x18½" |
| 2 arms | 2x6x28" |
| 2 small blocks | 1x1x3½" |

## CUTTING DIAGRAM

8-foot 1x6 ripped in half

| BACK SLAT | BACK SLAT | BACK SLAT | BACK SLAT | BACK SLAT | /// |
|---|---|---|---|---|---|
| BACK SLAT | BACK SLAT | BACK SLAT | BACK SLAT | SEAT SLAT | |

6-foot 1x6 ripped in half

| SEAT SLAT | SEAT SLAT | SEAT SLAT | /// |
|---|---|---|---|
| SEAT SLAT | SEAT SLAT | SEAT SLAT | /// |

6-foot 2x6

| ARM | ARM | ///// |
|---|---|---|

10-foot 2x4

| BACK SUPPORT | BACK SUPPORT | CROSS BRACE | FRONT LEG | //// |
|---|---|---|---|---|

10-foot 2x4

| SEAT SUPPORT | SEAT SUPPORT | CROSS BRACE | FRONT LEG | //// |
|---|---|---|---|---|

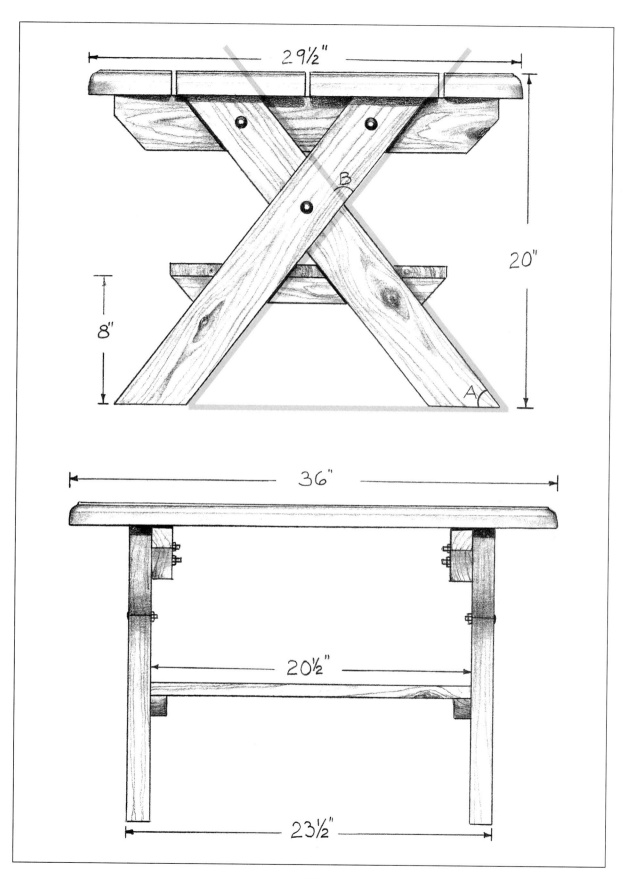

Sawbucks are the rough frames that people throw together to hold firewood logs while they cut them to stove length, and the sawbuck table gets reinvented every time someone takes lunch out to the person working on the woodpile and lays a board across the sawbuck to create a flat surface.

The appeal of the sawbuck construction for holding firewood is the crotch formed by the crossing legs. The V shape holds the wood, and the sawyer's downward push only tightens the grip. The appeal of the X-shaped legs for a table design lies in the fact that the legs form their own cross-bracing and do not require much help to keep them stable, which means that the tables are easy to build.

As simple as it is, however, the sawbuck table is one of the few pieces in this book that employs a traditional joint. Although the X of the legs could be formed by simply nailing two 2x4s in a cross, the weight from above would push on the legs as if it were pushing on a pair of levers. Eventually, the nails would twist right out. Another problem, as anyone building a sawbuck soon discovers, involves the difficulty of attaching supports for the tabletop if the two arms making the X do not line up with one another on a single plane.

A half-lap joint at the junction of the two arms of the X produces a very tight connection, with substantial wood surfaces bearing against one another to absorb the pressure from above. Half-lap joints also provide a large gluing surface and make bolting everything together simple. Finally, they line up the arms of the X so that the support for the top attaches easily.

The lower shelf on this table, while it provides a handy storage place for things like citronella candles and ashtrays, is not essential to the structure. It adds a bit of stability, but the table can stand without it.

1  Cut the legs to length, taking care that the angles of the cuts at the ends of the legs are consistent and match angle "a" on page 95.

2  Locate and lay out your half-lap joints with extreme care. Since you need two X-shaped assemblies, each with four free ends, any mistake that shortens one of those lengths will require as many as seven different additional cuts to get everything lined up again.

## HALF-LAP JOINT

To locate the joints, begin by measuring the exact width and thickness of the material you are using. Nowadays, a standard 2x4 measures 1½ or 1¾ by 3½ inches, but you will be lucky if things work out to a standard number, metric or imperial.

Divide the measurement for thickness in half, and keep that number in mind for the next step. Better yet, jot it down on a scrap of wood, and put that piece of wood right in the middle of your bench where you will not lose it.

3  Set out the four leg members on your bench, all aligned the same way. Measure exactly 8¼ inches down the length of each leg member from the point at the top end, and draw a line across each leg on the angle marked "b" on page 95. Now draw a second line parallel to the first and at a distance of exactly the width of your 2x4 material (approximately 3½ inches). You can use one of the legs to trace the second line. Half the wood between those lines must be removed to produce one side of the joint.

To determine how much wood to remove, extend the two lines down the sides of each 2x4 and mark the midway point through the thickness of the material (approximately ¾ inch).

All that's left to do now is to cut out the wood within those lines. As you do so, keep in mind that half laps should fit snugly. This is definitely a situation in which you should remind yourself

*A blow to the square edge of a tabletop leaves a mark. The same blow at the end of the board where the grain is exposed can knock a chunk of wood loose. You should, therefore, at least use a block plane to break the edges (see "Chamfering," page 75), and, especially if you decide to create an oval top for your sawbuck, you may want to round those edges with a router. A blunted edge survives wear and tear better and, at the same time, provides a more decorative and finished appearance.*

*The roundover profile—created by something called, not surprisingly, a roundover bit—makes the already substantial sawbuck tabletop look even heftier. Just as a fine sharp edge lends an air of lightness and delicacy to any piece of furniture, removing that edge produces the opposite effect.*

*You can use a ½-inch roundover bit or a full 1-inch roundover, with the bit set either flush, simply to smooth the corner, or ⅛ inch deeper to produce a slightly more complex profile. (See illustrations.)*

*If you own a selection of router bits, you may even want to experiment with some of the more elaborate edges such as Roman ogees or the standard panelling edge.*

*When you are routing a softwood such as pine, make numerous light passes rather than trying to hog away the whole amount in a single teeth-clenching swipe. If you cut too deeply along the side grain, you risk tearing away long wedge-shaped slivers. If you go too hard at the end grain, the whirling blade cannot keep*

*pace, so instead of cutting all the fibres, it grabs small hunks and wrenches them straight out from the end grain itself.*

*I know these things not because my router's manual says so, although it does, but as a consequence of my own impatience. Go slowly. And wear earplugs. They protect your hearing, but they also make it easier to remain calm while you wield your torquing, whining router, one of the most unnerving-sounding hand-held power tools known to humankind.*

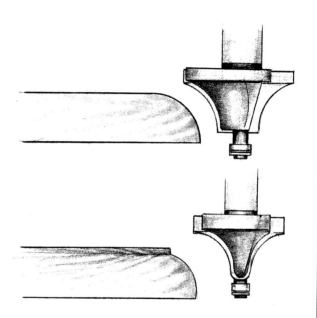

over and over about how much harder it is to put wood back than it is to remove it in the first place. Clamp your workpieces to the bench throughout the cutting and chiselling stages.

Using a handsaw, cut on the inside of your lines (a backsaw, dovetail saw or gentleman's saw is the right tool for this kind of work). You can even trace over your lines with a utility knife to create a tiny groove that will guide your first cuts. Saw down to just short of the depth line. Cut an X of the same depth across the material you want to remove, then chisel out the waste. Work from the edge of the wood toward the centre. Minor mistakes with the

cutting and chiselling disappear as long as the edges are cut true.

You can also cut a good half-lap joint using a circular saw if you take great care. To do this, follow the same procedure described on page 26 for making notches with a speed square; in this case, however, you will need an adjustable square to guide the saw. These heavy aluminum squares are sometimes called "squangles." Look for one at your local tool centre. Set the blade of the circular saw to cut just shy of the full depth you need, then use the adjustable square to guide your cuts. Ensure that the foot of the saw remains flat even as the blade cuts out the far side of the stock. Make several cuts between your lines to chew out the waste, then use a chisel to dress the joint and cut it to its full depth.

If you have a table saw, you can follow the same procedure and will probably get an even better result. If you know how to use a dado blade, you can make things that much easier again. A router also cuts good half-lap joints.

If you use a power tool to cut these joints, be sure to score the cut lines with a utility knife to prevent the blades from tearing clumps of wood fibres away from the finished edges.

4 Dry-fit the legs together, then pull them apart and spread lots of glue in the joint. Drill a single ⅜-inch hole all the way through. Unless your half-lap joint is perfect, which it needn't be for the table to be usable, it will be possible to wiggle the X. Take care, therefore, that the two Xs you make are at exactly the same angle before you fasten them. A couple of finishing nails will ensure that the angles are where you want them while you drive a ⅜-by-

## WEDGES

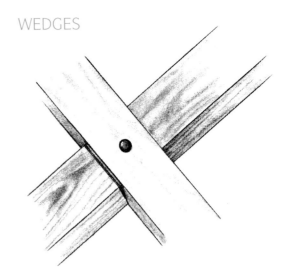

2½-inch carriage bolt through the hole and tighten. If you have made a hash of the half laps, this is the time to slip thin wedges into the joints to fill up any gaps. These will set in place with the glue, and any movement of the legs will only pinch them tighter in place.

## INSTALLING THE SHELF

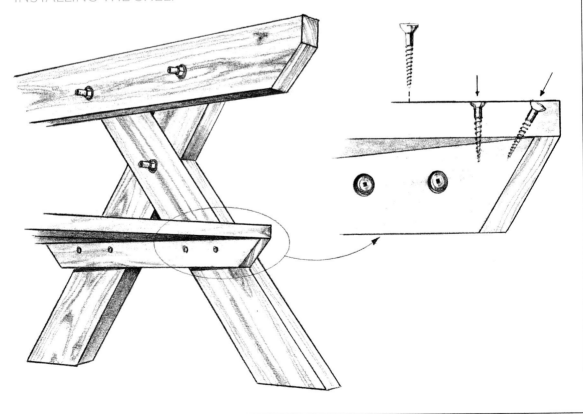

**5** If you used nails to steady everything in the previous stage, then you can carry on directly and install the top crosspieces. Drill holes, apply glue and install ⅜-by-4-inch carriage bolts. Again, some finishing nails can hold things in place while you fasten the pieces together. Be sure the two assemblies are identical.

**6** Install the supports for the lower shelf using #8 1¾-inch screws. Ensure that the lower shelf will be level by measuring down from the crosspiece at the top. Put everything aside to set.

**7** Cut the pieces for the lower shelf to exactly 20½ inches, and cut the top pieces to roughly 36 inches. Predrill the boards for the lower shelves with a countersink drill at approximately ½ inch from each end, three holes at the end of each board.

When the glue holding the Xs sets, attach the lower shelves to their supports with #8 1½-inch wood screws. If you have cut an angle on the ends of the shelf supports, take care not to screw through the bottom of the support; angle the end screw.

Attach the two outer shelf boards first, then centre the remaining 1x6 between them, leaving narrow gaps.

**8** At this point, you should have a free-standing frame lacking only the top. Centre the four 36-inch top pieces, and screw them down with countersunk #10 2½-inch wood screws.

**9** The only work still to be done depends on the shape you choose for the finished tabletop. You can true up the ends and leave it rectangular; you can cut off the corners to produce a stretched eight-sided shape; or you can make it rounded or oval.

## OVALS

To mark an oval on your table top, you need a pencil, a piece of string and two finishing nails. Begin by locating the exact centre of the table, then measure along the long axis the same distance in each direction and drive in the finishing nails. Tie the string into a loop large enough so that there is still plenty of slack when it is placed over the nails. Slip a pencil inside the string loop, and stretching the string as far as you can, trace out the oval.

Those are the essentials. Experiment to produce the precise shape you want, varying both the location of the nails on the long axis and the amount of slack in your string. Since the

TRACING ROUNDED ENDS

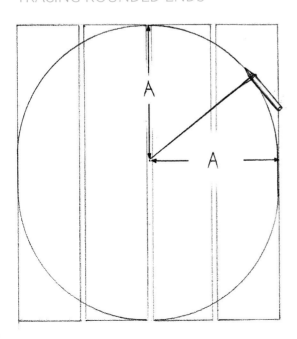

TRACING AN OVAL

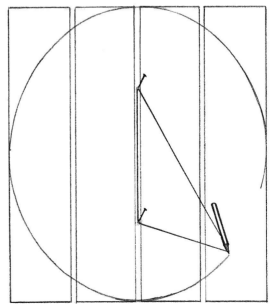

centre axis is actually a gap between boards, you may need to tack a piece of wood or cardboard in place so that you have somewhere to set the finishing nails.

## SIMPLE ROUNDED ENDS

This method for producing rounded ends on the sawbuck table does not make a proper oval, but it creates a larger finished surface.

Begin by making sure that the centre boards of the top overlap the supports by the same amount on each end (the other boards will be shortened and are not crucial). Measure the exact width of the tabletop as you have installed it; it should be approximately 29 or 30 inches. Divide that dimension by two. Now measure back from the ends along the long axis of the table, and mark that distance on the tabletop. Tie a piece of string to a pencil, then hold the other end of the string on the mark so that the pencil just reaches both to the sides of the table and to the end. Trace the radius onto the tabletop boards.

Cut the curves with a jigsaw or bow saw, true up the edges with your belt sander, and if you choose, finish them with a router.

# CUTTING DIAGRAM AND MATERIALS LIST

## MATERIALS LIST

one 10-foot 2x4
one 6-foot 2x4
two 6-foot 2x8s
one 6-foot 1x6

two ⅜"x2½" carriage bolts
four ⅜"x4" carriage bolts
1½" #8 wood screws
1¾" #8 wood screws
2½" #10 wood screws

## PARTS LIST

| | |
|---|---|
| 4 leg pieces | 2x4x28" |
| 2 arms | 2x4x24" |
| 4 top pieces | 2x8x36" |
| 3 shelf pieces | 1x6x20½" |
| 2 shelf brackets | 1x1½x17½" |

## CUTTING DIAGRAM

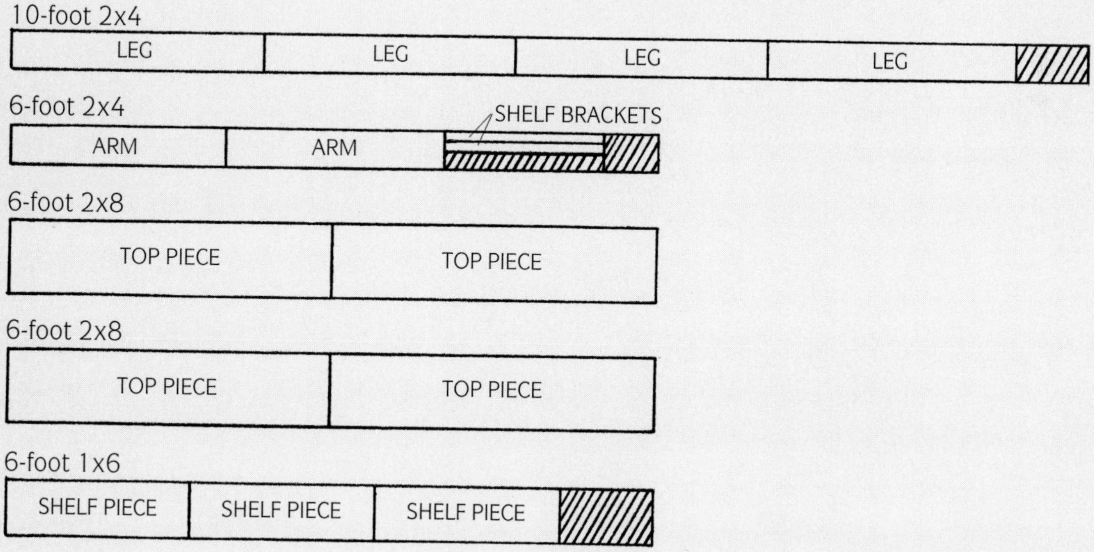

10-foot 2x4

| LEG | LEG | LEG | LEG | //// |
|---|---|---|---|---|

6-foot 2x4

SHELF BRACKETS

| ARM | ARM | ///// |
|---|---|---|

6-foot 2x8

| TOP PIECE | TOP PIECE |
|---|---|

6-foot 2x8

| TOP PIECE | TOP PIECE |
|---|---|

6-foot 1x6

| SHELF PIECE | SHELF PIECE | SHELF PIECE | ///// |
|---|---|---|---|

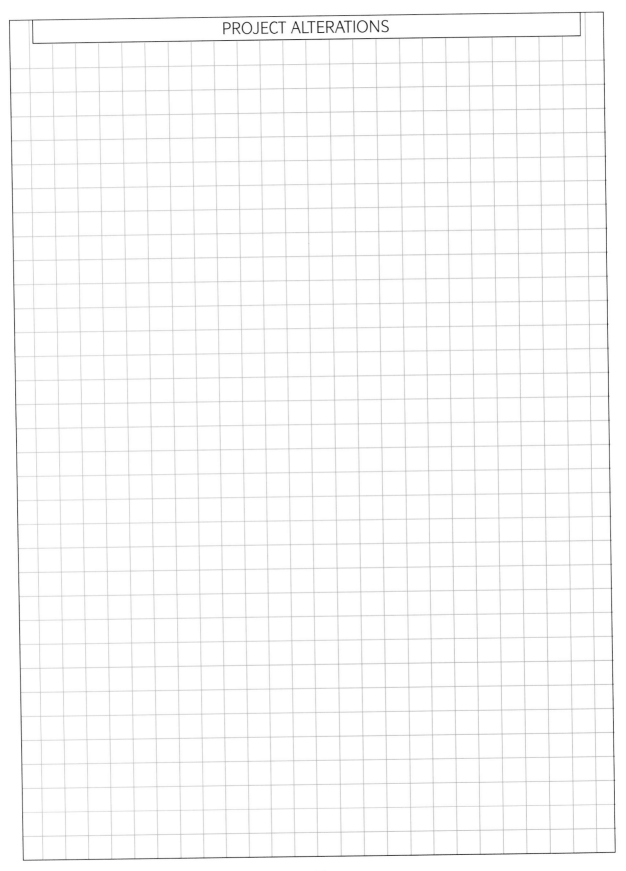

Plant stands are nothing more than butt-jointed boxes with tricky bits of decoration at the top and bottom. And when my shopmate Bob found me looking puzzled as I examined the crown moulding I'd bought, he offered advice for cutting the difficult compound angles necessary to fit the trim in place. "Take it across the parking lot to Terry's shop, and get him to do it on his mitre saw," he said. When I explained that I had to figure out a way to describe in writing how to cut compound mitres, he had the answer for that too, "Oh, well, tell people to take their trim across a parking lot, any parking lot, and find someone with a mitre saw to do it for them."

It is, when all is said and done, sage advice. The plant stand pictured opposite is made of plywood. Small blocks of wood brace the sides and also hold the top and bottom in place. Nothing could be easier; everything goes together quickly. Everything, that is, until you want to add the store-bought trim that gives the stands their appeal. There is no getting around it—cutting a 45-degree angle on the end of a piece of wood that is then installed at another, different angle to the vertical is a trick and a half. There is a good reason for designing a power tool specific to the task. Unfortunately, a plant stand is not a good enough excuse for going out and buying one.

Yet even though they do not justify more power tools, you still might have good reasons to build a plant stand or two. They decorate a deck or patio, introducing a vertical element in what is often a study in horizontal surfaces. They hold plants up out of the traffic zone of kids and dogs, and they can position plants in the sunlight. You can place them as you would a planter box to help divide a large expanse or to fill an empty corner. And since they are the only piece of outdoor furniture that owes anything at all to classical Greek architecture, a stand is bound to create conversation. Besides, once you succeed in installing the crown moulding to form the base and abacus of your wooden column, you will remain intrigued by how it all went together.

But first, the plywood column itself. In one important respect, the plans below reflect the fact that, in woodworking at least, discretion is often the better part of valour. The sides butt against one another rather than meeting in the corners at invisible mitre joints. While a mitre would be the superior method as far as appearance goes, such long mitres are impossible to cut without a table saw. As well, since even a perfect joint would open up after a while, you are better off avoiding the whole issue. Rely instead on careful finishing to hide the butt joint.

You can make these plant stand/columns in any dimensions you want, but length-to-width ratios of 2:1, 3:1 or 4:1 are best.

1   Begin by cutting the plywood lengths, with a table saw if you have one or using one of the methods described in "Cutting Plywood," page 109. Then cut 12 blocks of 2x2 stock approximately 4 inches long

It might appear better to cut two sizes of plywood so that you could glue and clamp everything at once by having the narrower side-pieces clamped between the wider ends. Since

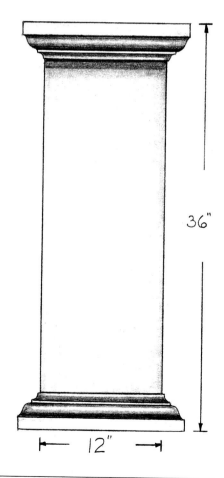

36"

12"

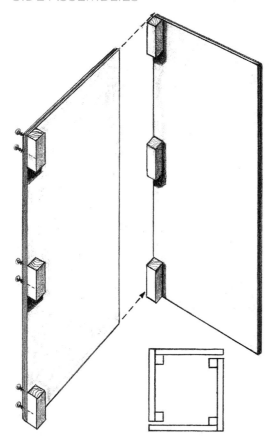

that you therefore have room to locate the top and bottom screws in such a way that they will be covered by the trim.

3  Before the glue sets, assemble the four pieces into two matching pairs of sides, two right angles. Spread glue along the edge of the plywood and on the blocks, then drive some 2½-inch finishing nails into the plywood to help hold things together while you screw them tight with #8 1¾-inch wood screws. Countersink the screw holes.

Drive screws into each of the blocks, but not into the end grain of the plywood. You will succeed only in splitting the laminations apart.

Check to be sure that the angle between the sides is exactly 90 degrees, and if you need to make corrections, loosen the screws slightly and tack a small brace across the ends (so the brace becomes the hypotenuse of the triangle it forms with the sides) to hold the two pieces in position while the glue sets.

Use furniture clamps to snug up the joint along the edge, but do not squeeze out all the glue. Place wooden blocks in the jaws of the clamps to prevent damage to the plywood.

Put everything aside while the glue sets.

4  Starting with the two pairs of sides you've assembled, there should be only one possible way to attach them so that they form a square column. Use lots of glue. Predrill and countersink the screw holes, and again use more finishing nails if you need to tack things in place as you work.

Once you have tightened everything down, check the diagonals at both ends to ensure that you have produced a perfectly square tube. It is surprisingly easy to build a long corkscrew twist into your columns, so peer at them every which way before you tighten the screws. Then, since the screws may not have drawn the pieces together along the entire length, snug the joints tight with furniture clamps placed in the spaces between the bracing blocks. Allow the glue to set.

5  To prepare for the next stage, cut the (provisional) top and bottom of the column. For now, the dimensions of these two identical squares will be equal to the outside dimensions of the column, plus the width of the crown moulding, plus some extra, say an inch or so.

you want to install bracing blocks at the four inside corners, however, it is just as easy to cut all the pieces the same and prepare four identical sidepieces. That way, you won't be likely to place the bracing blocks incorrectly, a mistake I made while building a prototype.

2  Glue and screw the blocks in place, three at one edge of each sidepiece. Centre one along the edge, and place the others *flush* with the ends. Drive two screws through from the outside of the plywood into each block, and countersink the heads. You could screw from the inside of the blocks into the plywood in order to hide the screws entirely, but since there will be other screwheads to deal with later, you gain little except a weaker connection. Remember, however, that the decorative crown moulding extends along the column at each end approximately 2 inches (depending on the size of the moulding you choose) and

(NOTE: The top and bottom pieces for the columns should be good thick slabs of plywood. If you don't have appropriate ¾-inch or 1-inch scraps around, ask your friends or scrounge at the lumberyard, where they probably have some odd bits you can buy for a good deal less than the cost of half a sheet of plywood. Otherwise, double up two pieces of ½-inch plywood.

6 When the glue has set, tack the top and bottom pieces in place with finishing nails driven into the corner bracing blocks. Do not bury the heads of the nails; you will want to pull them back out before you are done.

Now install the crown moulding. Do not take any measurements during this process; instead, establish all your cutting lines by holding the

## COMPOUND MITRES

*Abandon your tape measures for the duration of this task: they will betray you.*

*Mating any two pieces of wood to form a 90-degree outside angle requires forethought, care and luck. After all, you have to produce two identical 45-degree cuts while also ensuring that everything comes out to the right length. For those who haven't tried it, getting crown moulding around that same corner appears impossible. And after a couple of brain-bending hours spent grappling with the geometry of wood, many of us come away with that original suspicion intact. A thousand monkeys locked in a room with saws and crown moulding for a million years might come up with a proper outside mitre, but it obviously can't be done on purpose. Yet it can.*

*Crown moulding fills the 90-degree junction between two intersecting planes with a more decorative profile set at some other angle, and it's that "some other angle" which causes all the trouble. How on earth does one calculate the intersection of two different planes and then bisect that compound angle for the sharp 90-degree turn? How much math does it take?*

*The trick, however, is not to think about it at all: just set up your mitre box in such a way that it holds the crown moulding at the same angle as it will be mounted when installed. That is not as difficult as it sounds, because whatever angle the crown moulding follows—whether it slopes down at 60 degrees to the vertical or 45 degrees—it will always have two flat mounting surfaces on the back that are set at 90 degrees to each other.*

*Not coincidentally, the inside of your mitre box also has sides arranged at 90 degrees to one another. Once you visualize it, it's simple. All you need are a couple of strips of scrap either nailed or clamped to the inside of your mitre box so that when you slide a piece*

*of moulding into place under the saw guides, the two mounting surfaces align with the side and bottom of the box. That is the same position the crown moulding will take when you finally fasten it in place, and from that point on, you can just ignore the weird angle of the workpiece and carry on with the job of cutting the corner mitres, a job that will now be no more (or less) hair-raising than it usually is.*

*NOTES*

*1. You cannot save time by ignoring those extra strips mounted in the mitre box and simply holding the crown moulding at the proper angle with your free hand while you cut. You can try. You will not be happy with the result.*

*2. To establish the location of each cut you make, hold the moulding in place against the side of the square column of the plant stand and mark the shortest dimension directly onto the wood.*

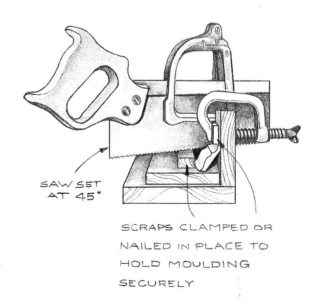

SAW SET
AT 45°

SCRAPS CLAMPED OR
NAILED IN PLACE TO
HOLD MOULDING
SECURELY

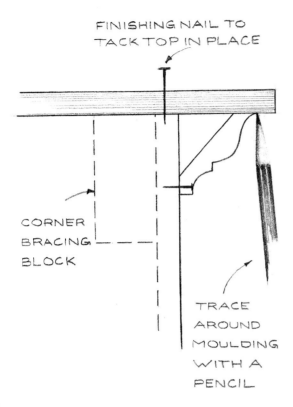

FINISHING NAIL TO
TACK TOP IN PLACE

CORNER
BRACING
BLOCK

TRACE
AROUND
MOULDING
WITH A
PENCIL

stock up to the workpiece and marking the lengths. Use glue to secure the mitred corners, and attach the moulding to the column with more glue and finishing nails, but *do not attach the moulding to the top and bottom pieces.* Once the crown is in place, trace a line around the crown moulding onto the top and bottom pieces and cut these to fit the moulding exactly. In your effort to make the mitres come together at the corners of the moulding, you may have created something other than a perfect square, and this is a way to accommodate that slight imperfection. Attach the top and bottom with plenty of glue on the corner blocks as well as on the edge of the column plywood and the edge of the moulding. Drive #8 2½-inch screws down into the corner blocks, and

use finishing nails to pin the moulding in place while the glue sets.

7 If you do not want the edge of the plywood to show, trim the top and bottom with strips of scrap or with plywood edging available at the lumberyard. Glue and nail these in place.

8 Finally, if you have access to a router—perhaps the person who did your compound mitre cuts for you has one—you may choose to use a ¼-inch cove bit to cut a flute into each of the four long corner edges of the column itself. Do this last, because you do not want to run these detail cuts down the entire length of the edges, and if you wait until the crowns are installed, the base of the router will come to the edge of the moulding and stop you at the right place. (See illustration, page 105.)

## FINISHING

Since the finished column or plinth or plant stand (however you prefer to think of it) should be painted, there is no need to build it from expensive good-one-side plywood. Rough exterior grade, with its more moisture-resistant glue, will do fine, and you can prepare it for a smooth final finish with some drywall compound or car body filler or any of the more durable powdered compounds for repairing plaster and Sheetrock walls. First, give the whole piece a quick sanding and apply a coat of filler. I used drywall compound from the bottom of a 5-gallon bucket that the previous tenant had left in the shop space I was renting. I squeegeed it liberally over the finished stand with a 4-inch putty knife, filling every crevice and crack and line in the wood grain. I let it dry for a couple of days and used a large sanding block to produce as flat a surface as possible. By the time I finished sanding, almost none of the compound remained, but the surface was as even as could be. I tidied up around the moulding and flutes by hand, then covered everything with a high-quality sealer/primer before applying the final colours.

Reaching across a sheet of plywood as you cut along a pencil line with a circular saw scores high on the danger index. It also does a pitiful job. No matter how slowly and carefully you go, the difference between what you want and what you get will resemble the difference between a divided highway and a lakeshore drive. Unless, of course, you take steps to force your saw to travel a straight line.

To do so, you need a stable work surface: two sturdy sawhorses and a level floor are a start. If the sawhorses are narrow, it may be necessary to nail a 2x4 across the top of each to make a broader support. Then lay the plywood down, and consider your needs.

If you want to cut a narrow strip from the sheet, the cleverest trick I know comes from a **Fine Homebuilding** "Tips & Techniques" column. Take a pair of stair gauges—tiny finger-tightened screw jaws designed to be fixed onto a rafter square so that you can mark the rise and run on stair stringers—and attach them to the back and front of the base of your circular saw. With

the saw unplugged, measure carefully from the edge of the blade, and set the gauges up in line with the width you want to cut from the sheet. Then just make sure the gauges stay firmly against the factory edge of the sheet as you cut. (See illustration.)

The width of the saw's base limits the stair-gauge trick to cutting narrow strips from the edges of the factory sheet. All other cuts require that you spend more time getting ready to cut than actually cutting, but if you want to navigate the open expanse of a 4x8, preparation is essential. Only a guide clamped firmly in place will ensure a straight cut.

Since the cut you make can be only as good as the guide you follow, it's best to use a milled straightedge or the factory-perfect side of a piece of sheet stock. If you cut across the 4-foot dimension, for example, you can clamp a mason's level in place and use that. Take an exact measurement from the edge of the saw's cutting teeth to the edge of the saw base, then mark the position of the guide by measuring back from the line that marks the cut you want to make.

Clamp the level in place gently—it's a precision tool that should be handled with respect—and as you make your cut, be sure to keep the base of the saw tight against the level. It is remarkably easy, with all the noise and concern about keeping the cord free, to stray from your path as you stretch out across the plywood.

For cutting 8-foot lengths, people often keep a strip cut from the edge of a full sheet of plywood to use as a longer guide. (Note: An 8-foot piece of lumber often has twists and curves. Dimensionally stable sheet materials work far better.) If you find yourself cutting a lot of sheets, there are permanent guides that you can buy or make.

## MATERIALS LIST

one-half sheet ½" plywood
two 8-foot pieces cornice moulding
two 16"x16" scraps of ¾"-1" plywood
twelve small blocks from scrap 2x2x4" (approx.)
*optional:*
two 8-foot ½x1s

1¾" #8 wood screws
2½" #8 wood screws
1" finishing nails
2½" finishing nails

## PARTS LIST

| | |
|---|---|
| 4 side pieces | 11½"x36"x½" plywood |
| 8 moulding pieces | do not precut |
| 2 end pieces | 16"x16"x¾"-1" plywood |
| 12 small blocks | 2x2x4" (approx.) |
| *optional:* | |
| 8 trim pieces | ½x1x18" |

## CUTTING DIAGRAM

Half sheet ½" plywood

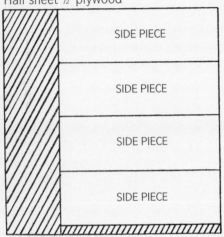

8-foot cornice moulding

8-foot cornice moulding

8-foot ½x1 for trim pieces

8-foot ½x1 for trim pieces

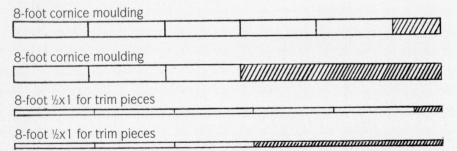

Almost everyone who heard about this book eventually led me out the back door of their house to some treasured piece of deck furniture and suggested I include it. Tables, chairs, homegrown benches, sundry whatsits and furniture facsimiles, each weathered piece was doing its outdoor job and looking as permanent as the deck itself. Of these backyard favourites, only the tray and stand described below made the final cut—none of the rest were as useful or as pleasing or as well suited to their tasks.

Friends of mine own one of these table/tray/stands. It gets regular use all summer long, and even though it is probably a semiprecious antique, when it began to show signs of wear last year, they added a coat of paint. It continues to serve and stand and wait.

People who entertain on the deck or lawn need something with which to carry loads of dip and drinks—a tray of some sort. And anyone carrying a loaded tray needs a place to put it down—a stand. Beyond these minimal functions, however, both items should be unobtrusive and easy to set out of the way. The following plans satisfy all the requirements. The stand folds away to almost nothing, and some découpage or stencils or the efforts of a talented painter friend can transform the tray into just the kind of decoration that belongs in the kitchen or on a cottage wall.

You need access to a table saw for this project, because you need small-dimension hardwood in order to build it. Few lumberyards nowadays carry small pieces; many do not even carry the large pieces in standard dimen-

sions. In their hardwood section, they stock lengths anywhere from 2 feet to 10 feet and in sizes ranging from a standard ¾-inch plank to something 4⅞ inches thick at one end and 4¹³⁄₁₆ at the other. Hardwoods cost too much to dress down to standard dimensions. Therefore the most difficult part of building this set will be standing in front of a pile of variously sized birch and cherry and oak and maple chunks trying to figure out how to cut all the members you need from the smallest possible piece of wood, keeping in mind that every saw cut costs you ⅛ inch. If you don't own a table saw, here's an excuse to buy one. Of course, you'll have to overlook the fact that most lumberyards will do the cutting for you if you know exactly what you want and are willing to pay a small hourly shop rate.

Having decided this project should be made from hardwood and thereby having forced you to go through all the head scratching necessary to get your materials, I next simplified the original design of the stand in a way that will return all that time to you. The tray stand that inspired this design set the pivot point for the folding legs closer to one end of the legs than the other. It also included two angled cuts on the top of each leg—one where the leg met the tray bottom, and the other where the leg met the lip on the edge of the tray—and only one cut at the bottom of each leg where it rested against the floor. These two features, combined with the requirements that one pair of legs has to fit within the other pair and that the heads of the bolts should show at each end of the fin-

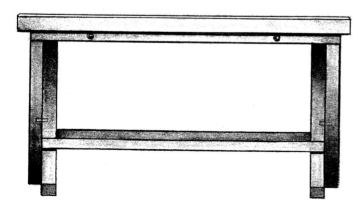

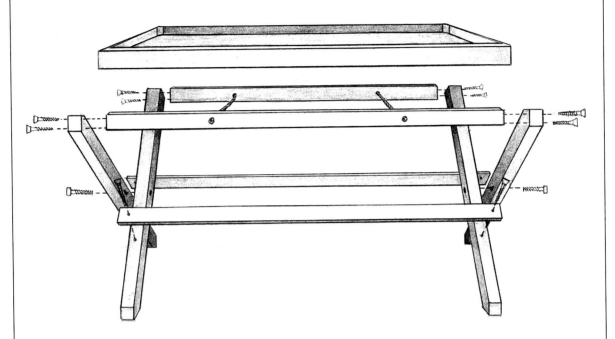

ished stand, meant that there were at least a dozen incorrect ways to assemble the legs. A seemingly straightforward task quickly gained the complexity of a Rubik's cube.

By moving the pivot point to the centre of each leg and making two cuts on both ends of each leg—in other words, by making everything symmetrical—I eliminated all but a couple of the potential errors and significantly increased the likelihood of the project actually being completed within the patience allotted.

## THE STAND

1 Begin by cutting all your stock to the needed dimensions. Note: As with many of the projects in this book, you can modify the size of the materials you use and change the overall size of the finished piece. However, you need to take greater care in this case, since the finished width of the tray and the finished width of the tops of the legs need to mate exactly and in such a way that the outside edge of the top of each leg is perfectly vertical. The tray sits firmly on the stand because its weight forces the legs tight against the lip on the underside of the tray.

2 After cutting the materials, locate the centre point of each leg. Do this before you cut angles on the legs for the simple reason that you will have less trouble keeping the tape measure hooked over the squared ends. Drill ¼-inch holes at each centre point, and use ¼-by-2½-inch carriage bolts to assemble the two pairs of legs so that you can double-check the location of the holes. Disassemble the legs again, and cut two 45-degree angles on each end of all four legs. Each finished leg should have pointed ends, and the overall length from tip to tip should still be the full 21¾ inches. Save the small triangular off-cuts that you produce while trimming the ends of the legs.

3 Attach one leg to each end of the two 1x1 crosspieces to form two pairs of leg assemblies. Since you are working with hardwood, take great care. In these small dimensions, it can split, and screws can break when driven into hardwood. Predrill countersunk ¹⁄₁₆-inch pilot holes, and spread some epoxy glue before gently driving home two #6 1½-inch wood screws to connect the legs and crosspieces. The sides of the crosspieces must line up with the 45-degree angles on the ends of the legs.

4 Before the glue sets, slide the leg assemblies together (one inside the other) and ensure that everything fits properly and that the legs scissor open and closed freely. Only then install the lower ¼-by-1-inch crosspieces. It will be easier to slip the leg assemblies together without the lower braces tightened in place and easier to know where the lower pieces belong once you see which way the leg assembly folds. Attach the lower braces approximately 5 or 6 inches up from the bottom of the legs with more glue. Securing them with a screw at each end while the glue sets is optional; alternatively, you can use a couple of small finishing nails or clamps.

## THE TRAY

The original tray in this set came equipped with handles made by turning up the ends of the tray a couple of inches and cutting a wide slot for a grip. They looked awkward, however, and they represented another complication in the cutting of materials for the tray. After building a couple of prototypes, one with handles and one without, I found that it was far easier to set the tray down without handles, since I could just slide my hand along to the corners to guide the tray and stand together. If you feel you must have handles for the tray, buy some brass ones at a hardware store and fasten them onto the finished ends. Tray handles are the ones that angle up slightly so that your fingers do not get pinched when you set the tray on a flat surface.

1 To assemble the tray, you need two 3-foot furniture clamps and some more epoxy glue. Lay out the pieces so that the ends butt inside the sides, and when you have everything ready, apply glue and set up the clamps. Check the diagonals immediately to ensure that all four corners are 90 degrees. After the glue sets—and if you've used 5-minute epoxy, give it 20 minutes—gently remove the clamps and measure the inside dimensions of the frame. They should be 16 inches by 29¾ inches, so that is the size of ¼-inch plywood you need.

2 Prepare the frame by installing the ½-by-¼-inch strips around the inside and flush with the bottom of the larger members. These,

too, can be glued in place and secured with ¾-inch brads. Apply the glue liberally in the corners, where it will provide additional strength.

3 Having built a lip around the inside of the tray frame, lay the plywood in place, spreading glue to fix it and tacking it down with brads. Now retrieve the small triangular pieces that you cut from the ends of the legs, and se-

CORNER DETAIL, TOP VIEW

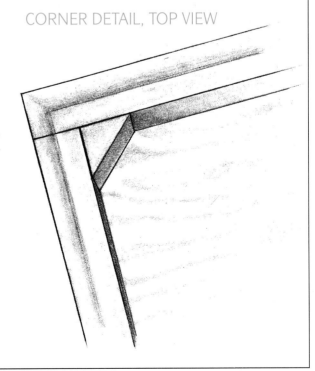

## CLAMPS

*Nothing beats finding tools: finding chisels on sale, finding a full set of sockets at a flea market or auction. Certainly, nothing could beat finding bar clamps in the abandoned workshop across the hall from where I was building the projects contained in this book. They were so caked with rust that I had to use a belt sander to uncover the actual bars. I found four of them, and after several hours' work, they doubled the number of full-sized furniture clamps available in our little shop. The total: eight bar clamps, about a dozen assorted C-clamps, one surprisingly handy Quik-clamp (which tightens by means of a giant trigger so that it can be used one-handed), two wooden clamps (or "wooden handscrews," as they are sometimes called) and several homemade wooden clamps. (See "Homemade Clamps and Presses," page 69.)*

*This collection begins to approach the minimum number of clamps any shop should contain, and if there is one piece of woodworking advice that endures, it is, "Go out and buy another clamp." When in doubt, buy a clamp. When you have nothing else to do in the hardware store, buy a clamp. And when you're stuck on a project, reach for a clamp and figure out how it could simplify your problem.*

*Building furniture is never anything more than cutting wood into pieces and then sticking them together. Clamps have a role at every step. It is often a very good idea to clamp a piece of wood to the bench for cutting. It is **always** a good idea to clamp pieces together while you install the fasteners and let the glue set.*

*And be sure to buy a web clamp, because once you own one, you'll find uses for it, beginning with the harvest table on page 56. When you first position the legs around the apron assembly, a web clamp will hold everything in place while you look it over and make your marks.*

lecting the four best, use more epoxy to fix them in the corners, where they will hold the plywood in place and also help strengthen the corners and keep them square. Do not trim the extra from these small braces until the glue sets completely.

At this stage, if you have followed all the directions scrupulously, when the legs of the stand sit flat on the floor, the width of the tops of the legs should exactly match the 15½-inch space on the underside of the tray. If anything has gone wrong, you will have to adjust some or all of the angled cuts on the legs and perhaps even plane the top crosspieces. Finish all the adjustments, and only then install the braided polyester cord.

The cords should be slightly stretchy. You want them to hold the legs so that the top crosspieces are a fraction of an inch closer together than the full width. That way, it will be easy to set the tray in place, but the weight of the load will be able to scissor the legs tight against the lip on the underside of the tray, locking everything in place. Drill two ⅛-inch holes through each crosspiece, and countersink a larger opening to provide a recess for the knots. Fiddle with the knots until you get the lengths of cord just right.

Finishing the tray and stand is not as crucial as with some outdoor furniture. The whole unit weighs only a few pounds and folds and stores away easily. If, however, you expect to leave it outside all summer as a kind of coffee table, apply layers of primer and paint and consider drilling some drainage holes through the bottom of the tray. But if you plan to store the tray and stand inside, your options range from furniture wax to delicate antiquing milk paints. I finished one version I built with a bright scarlet stain that I wiped off while it was still wet to produce a faint red finish, which I then polyurethaned.

## MATERIALS LIST

The parts for the tray and stand can easily be cut from a piece of hardwood measuring 1 ½ inches by 3½ inches by 8 feet. They can also be cut from a 1x6x8' or from innumerable combinations of smaller pieces. Because there is no way to know what awaits you at the lumberyard, there is no way to recommend what you should buy or how you should cut it. You will just have to join the other people at the hardwood rack who are scratching their heads over similar problems. Please note: The dimensions given are not nominal. The legs, for example, should measure 1 inch by 1½ inches.

two ¼"x2½" carriage bolts
1½" #6 wood screws
small brads
4' braided polyester cord

## PARTS LIST

Stand:
| | |
|---|---|
| 4 legs | 1"x1½"x21¾" |
| 1 upper crosspiece | 1"x1"x27⅛" |
| 1 upper crosspiece | 1"x1"x25⅛" |
| 1 lower crosspiece | ¼"x1"x27¼" |
| 1 lower crosspiece | ¼"x1"x29½" |

Tray:
| | |
|---|---|
| 2 sides | ½"x1½"x30⅞" |
| 2 ends | ½"x1½"x16" |
| 2 inside strips | ¼"x½"x30¾" |
| 2 inside strips | ¼"x½"x15½" |
| 1 tray surface | ¼" plywood 16"x29¾" |

## CUTTING DIAGRAM

Unlike the other projects in this book, there is no "best" way to cut the pieces for the tray and stand. Other possibilities than the one shown here may be more appropriate. Pieces that are shown being cut from an 8-foot length, for example, could just as easily be cut from two 4-foot lengths. Price the pieces available at your lumberyard.

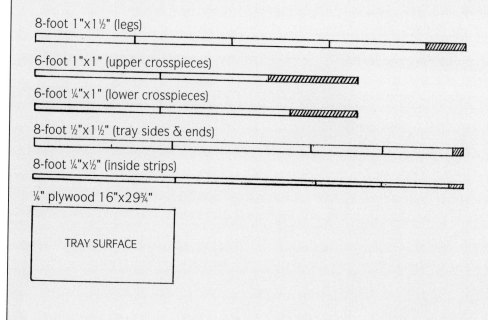

8-foot 1"x1½" (legs)

6-foot 1"x1" (upper crosspieces)

6-foot ¼"x1" (lower crosspieces)

8-foot ½"x1½" (tray sides & ends)

8-foot ¼"x½" (inside strips)

¼" plywood 16"x29¾"

TRAY SURFACE

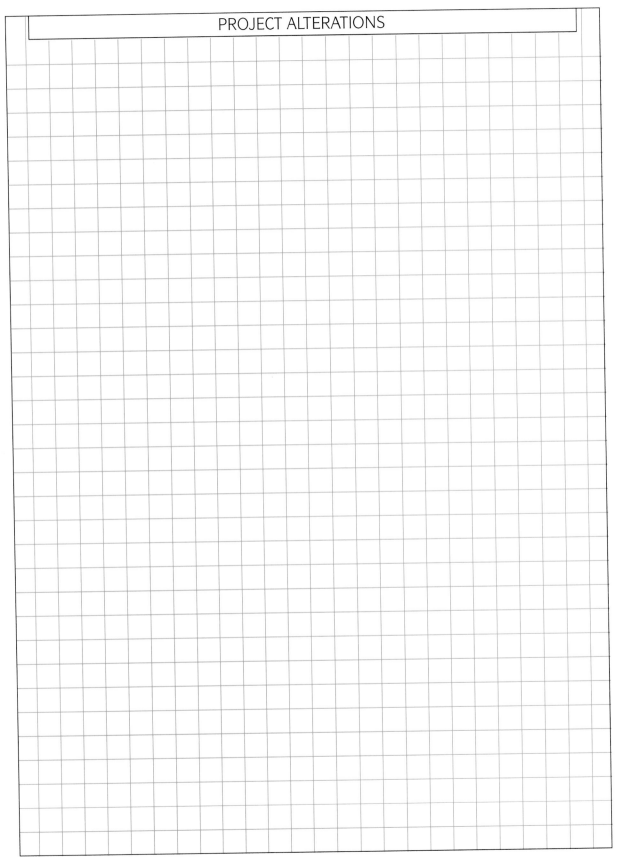

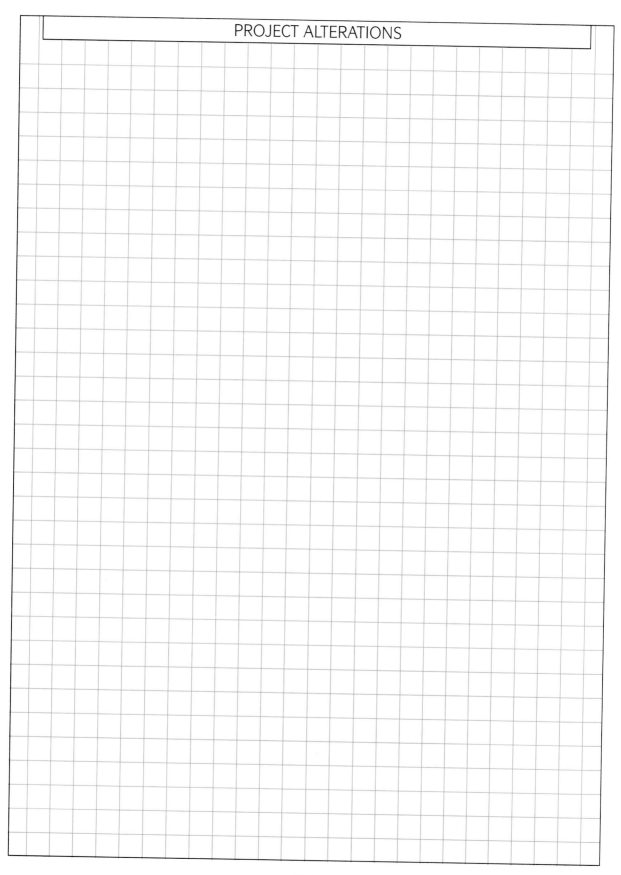

PROJECT ALTERATIONS

The first sawhorses I ever built remain a graphic reminder to me that there is always more than one way to get something wrong. They are not so useless as to deserve destruction, but they don't do a good job of any of the things sawhorses should do. They wobble from side to side and front to back. They are too tall, and they do not stack for storage, so they always take up twice as much floor space as they should. And their tops aren't wide enough.

My friend Jeff, on the other hand, knows how to make lovely sawhorses. He learned when he apprenticed with a master carpenter, who had probably been taught by an earlier generation. Those unnamed woodworkers had no doubt learned during their apprenticeships, and so on. The design has the feel of having been gotten right a long time ago.

There is also a wonderful story that goes with Jeff's sawhorse design; if you care to look it up, he published it in *Country Journal* in 1987. But here are the essentials of the design.

1 Set out a 6-foot 2x6 or 2x8 fir, pine or pressure-treated top board, then tilt the shoe of your power saw to the angle shown on this page (15 degrees). If your saw came with a fence attachment, use it to cut up and down the length of the board on the same side. If you don't have a fence attachment, simply measure in a minimal amount (say, ¼ inch) from each edge, and use a straightedge or a chalk line to mark two lines down the length of the board. Cut along the lines with the shoe of the saw tilted.

No matter which method you use, you should end up with a board that is 6 feet long and slightly narrower on the top side than on the bottom. Leave the shoe of the saw set at an angle—you'll need it for Step 4.

2 Lay out two pieces of 8-foot 1x6 side by side. You really should have a sawhorse for this step, but you don't. Of course, while you consider what to do in the meantime, you can reflect on the fact that if you did not *want* a pair of sawhorses in the first place, you would not now *need* a pair of sawhorses. Your motive for making these horses has now doubled, at least until you finish them. And if, in order to *make* the sawhorses, you find some substitute for sawhorses, perhaps you won't want to make them anymore.

3 Pencil three lines on each board, marking out a total of four legs. To do so, use the same setting of the sliding T-bevel you used to set the shoe of the saw, and transfer that angle to the top of the 1x6s so that the two long points of each leg are both inside the 36-inch length. (See illustration, page 122.)

## CUTTING ANGLES

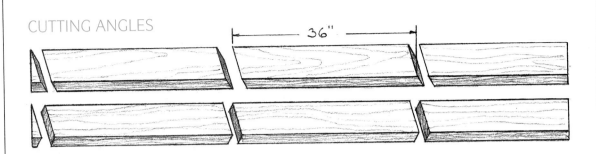

36"

4 Now comes the clever part of the explanation that Jeff gave in his *Country Journal* instructions. With the shoe of the saw still set at an angle, make the first two cuts from one side of the boards, "then *walk around to the other side and cut from there* for the next two. That will reverse the slant of the compound angle. Each *pair* of legs cut this way will be identical and will be at opposite corners of the sawhorse diagonally." If you follow these instructions exactly, you will get just what you need. If you try to achieve the same result in any other way, you are guaranteed to pass into confusion, and you are not certain to emerge. Follow the illustrations carefully, and do not even try to understand them

until you have the pieces in your hands. At that point, the way everything fits together will be self-evident.

5 Repeat Steps 3 and 4 with the other two 1x6s, but set these four legs aside, and don't even think about getting them mixed up with the first four. Now straighten up the shoe of your power saw, and cut the 2x6 or 2x8 top piece in half so that you have two identical 3-foot-long tops, one for each set of legs.

6 Set four legs against one of the tops so that the ends of the legs come out flat on the floor and flush with the top of the sawhorse. Position them so that each leg is about 6 inches from the end of the top board. Fasten the legs in place with 2-inch galvanized ardox nails.

## THE GROANING BOARD

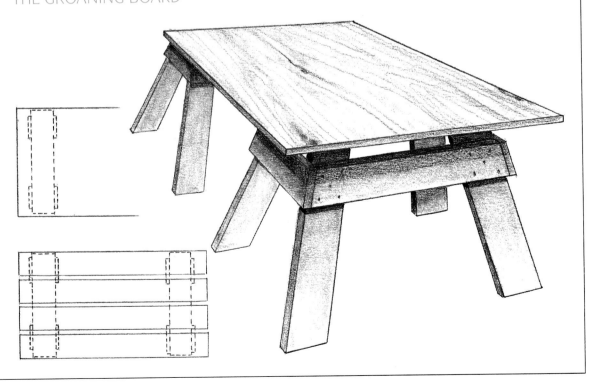

7 Using more 2-inch galvanized nails, fasten the side gussets in place first and then the end gussets. You can trim them to fit as you go, but all your lines should still match the same angle you started with.

## THE GROANING BOARD

If you have everyone you know over for a barbecue once a year, you need a groaning board, a huge surface on which to spread bowls of potato salad and charbroiled meats. This table would ideally be sturdy enough to trust with a large crowd milling around and would store away for the rest of the year, and its constituent parts would have other uses. That is where a pair of sawhorses comes in handy. Once you have two horses, a substantial table is only a sheet of plywood or a few 2-inch boards and a couple of drill holes away.

1 If you have a sheet of ¾-inch plywood or 2-inch boards, set the horses so that the tops are 6 to 7 feet apart, then position the plywood or boards on top.

2 Use a 1-inch hole saw to drill through the top material and through the sawhorse top beneath it. Drill one hole in each end of a 2-inch board or, if you use a sheet of plywood, two holes at each end.

3 Cut lengths of 1-inch dowel so that each is an inch or so longer than the total thickness of the top of the sawhorse and the plywood or top boards. Rig up each dowel so that it cannot slip all the way through the holes: you can do this by drilling a small hole in the dowel near one end and inserting a short length of smaller dowel in it or by just wrapping some tape at one end.

4 Line up the boards or plywood and the sawhorses, and tap the dowels into place. If you use boards, the whole structure will be firm but will be able to wiggle a little bit. If you use a single sheet of plywood, it will be remarkably sturdy. (Note: The 4-foot width of a piece of plywood is a bit much for a table. If you can cut it down to 3 feet, it will seem a more comfortable and familiar dimension.)

## MATERIALS LIST (for two sawhorses)

one 6-foot 2x6
four 8-foot 1x6s
two 6-foot 1x6s

2" galvanized ardox nails

## PARTS LIST (for two sawhorses)

| | |
|---|---|
| 2 top pieces | 2x6x36" |
| 8 legs | 1x6x36" |
| 4 side gussets | 1x6x34" |
| 4 end gussets | 1x6x16" |

## CUTTING DIAGRAM

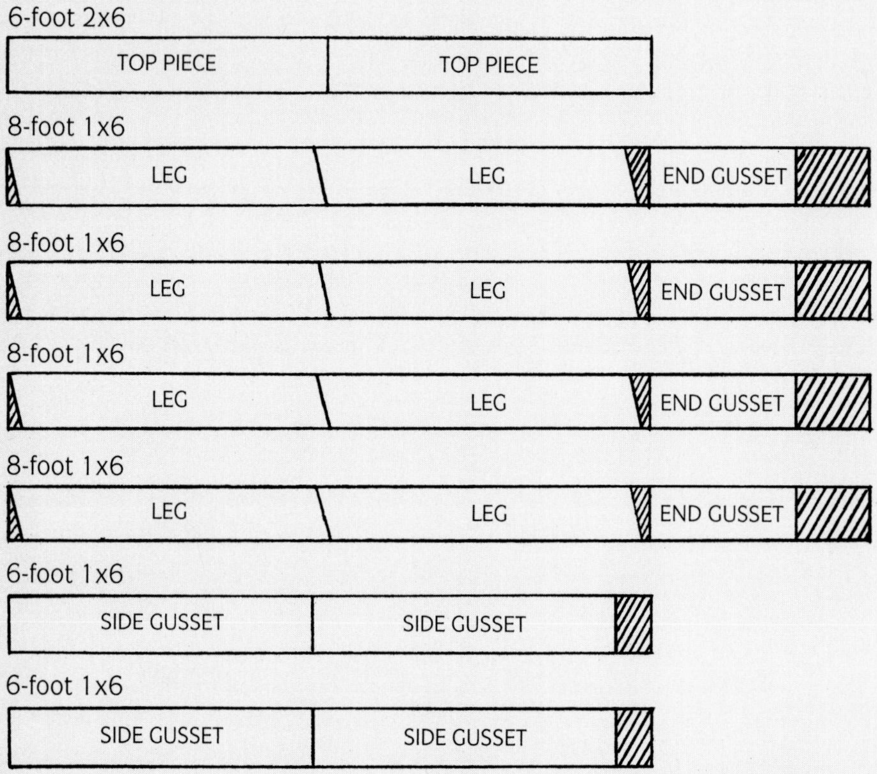

6-foot 2x6

| TOP PIECE | TOP PIECE |
|---|---|

8-foot 1x6

| LEG | LEG | END GUSSET |
|---|---|---|

8-foot 1x6

| LEG | LEG | END GUSSET |
|---|---|---|

8-foot 1x6

| LEG | LEG | END GUSSET |
|---|---|---|

8-foot 1x6

| LEG | LEG | END GUSSET |
|---|---|---|

6-foot 1x6

| SIDE GUSSET | SIDE GUSSET |
|---|---|

6-foot 1x6

| SIDE GUSSET | SIDE GUSSET |
|---|---|

# INDEX